CONFRON.

written by Peter Howe

TO Karen,

Keep fighting the good fight,
I wish you all the best.

Regards,

Peter Howe

ALSO BY THIS AUTHOR

The Game Changer: A Collection of Poetry

CONFRONT THE RAVEN

written by Peter Howe

PRINTED BY CREATESPACE, AN AMAZON.COM COMPANY
CREATESPACE, CHARLESTON SC

FIRST PRINTING, 2016

ISBN-13: 978-1537235042
ISBN-10: 1537235044

DEDICATIONS

In life it is easy to dream, it is a lot harder to chase them until they come true, and knowing there are people who will support your pursuit can make all the difference. I would like to thank those people, my mother and sister, I would like to thank my best friends Stephen, Stacey and Fran who have been extremely supportive. The older brother I never had Steven Reid and my other friends Rob, Steven and Chris who always have my back. I would like to thank the people from my former workplace The Manor who were so supportive when my first book came out and have been encouraging every step of the way with this project. Finally, I would like to dedicate this book to everyone else who believes in a better world and knows that getting there won't be easy but it will be worth it.

I would also like to give a special thanks to Jen from Heartisan Creations for her hard work designing to help bring my idea for the cover to life and helping design the interior.

TABLE OF CONTENTS

TABLE OF CONTENTS
Stories

INTRODUCTION

I hope you enjoy this book, if you have not read my previous book, *The Game Changer: A Collection of Poetry*, feel free to check it out and I hope you enjoy my future books as well. This book is a collection of 16 poems and 16 stories some are short others are not so short stories. I hope you will consider some of the ideas that will be raised in this book and perhaps even see the world differently. While some of the topics in this book might get intense I hope that you are willing to ride it out and extract the reason from the madness and find hope even in the depths of despair.

Poems

I RESPECTFULLY DISAGREE

I took a stroll down memory lane, last year late December,
it was as innocent and funny, as I remember,

The Muppet's Christmas Carol, a wonderful nostalgic trip,
most of it was great, but a terrible thing did slip,

It was the joyous song, as the movie reached its end,
"If you want to know, the measure of a man, you simply count his friends",

This took me by surprise, a terrible way to test,
the most popular people, are rarely in fact the best,

How many people have friends, only because they are rich,
or because of the power they wield, even if they're a bastard or bitch,

How many people, who have a heart of gold,
are rejected superficially, by the shallow and the cold,

Throw Facebook in there, and the numbers become a joke,
people you don't even like, you will never meet these folks,

So measure people differently, how about character and actions,
this may bother some people's beliefs, but I shake my head at these factions,

Popularity doesn't equal greatness, I hope you now see,
why I say to this film I love, I respectfully disagree.

THE MOMENT

Imagine having a hero, who everyone thinks is gold,
maybe they are recent, or a legend of old,

All of a sudden, you stumble across uncomfortable facts,
they weren't a hero at all, they were villainous with impact,

Maybe you only have a minute, to make up your mind,
perhaps you've had a few days, to handle the truth that is unkind,

So you come face to face, the moment has come at last,
where you can either smash or uphold, the misconceptions of the past,

But imagine if this hero, is the one they love and revere,
that shattering the illusion, would leave many with tears,

Heartbroken and disappointed, their inspiration has fallen,
leaving the masses, angry, cynical and sullen,

For some the choice is easy, just go with the flow,
for others the choice is easy, the people must know,

When faced with the choice, the best have cowered and ran,
many couldn't pull the trigger, from Lisa Simpson to Batman,

Eventually the lie will fall, it is only a matter of time,
delaying the inevitable, hoping the myth will be past its prime,

Who will inspire those, that need someone to look up to,
what hero could replace the old, and inspire greatness anew,

The answer won't come quickly, there will be a backlash it's true,
the answer is when the moment comes, it could be you,

A hero isn't perfect, but can be one for exposing frauds,
after all is it not heroic, to tell the truth against all odds?

PEN AND THE SWORD

His name is Mohammed, from parallel realities,
a place with similar joy, and similar fatalities,

In both his father was killed, the smart bomb wasn't so clever,
in both it turned a key, it threw open a lever,

Of rage and anger, how dare they kill my dad,
he was an honourable man, hardly anything bad,

Then the split occurs, one picks up a sword,
one buys pens and paper, with what little he can afford,

The warrior decides, that vengeance will be bred,
as the dry, brown, sand turns wet and red,

The other writes his fury, but also restraint and peace,
he doesn't want others to suffer loss, the stranger or his niece,

The warrior is eventually killed, the sword's not as mighty as the gun,
while the writer is only watched, he is an admired one,

Finally decades later, the writer is now a legend,
the man who decided, to stand and defend,

The higher ground, the place where the righteous preside,
who help pull those on the fence, onto the peaceful side,

Because the writer realized, any fool can swing a sword,
but it takes courage, to write what can't be ignored.

THANK YOU MY ᖴRIEND

I started seeing flashes, of my gruesome demise,
as my will to forge on was dying, this secret behind my eyes,

Things weren't getting better, more frustration every day,
no end in sight, things improve, no way,

Certain lyrics stuck to my heart, my life as it was seeming,
"seems like it's never gonna change, you must be dreaming,"

Sum 41 said it well but Rise Against said it better,
how I felt, right down to the letter,

"I don't want to be here anymore, be here anymore,
I know there's nothing left worth staying for,
your paradise is something I've endured,

I don't think I can fight his anymore,
I'm listening with one foot out the door,
and something has to die to be reborn,
I don't want to be here anymore,"

As those thoughts became stronger, I finally knew my ultimatum,
choose an unpredictable life, or the predictable death to come,

I had one key question to ask myself, was my life worth the leap,
was I prepared to stay alive, to dive into uncertainty so deep,

I fought with myself about that, all the damage rejection had done,
I finally realized, the two things that matter a tonne,

First is what I would say to others, about their human value,
everyone deserves the chance to be happy, that includes you,

The second thing was more personal, I looked hard at the things I write,
I had things to say, something worthy of the fight,

I reached the point when I said enough, that time was going to end,
I would move onto something else, and give myself time to mend,

Choosing life is hard, when you can't imagine what you will face,
and when you look in your in-box for replies, and all you see is blank space,

But I chose life nonetheless, and I shoved the weight off my shoulders,
that I had allowed to become so big, the weight of large boulders,

I had a new purpose, publish my thoughts the Game Changer,
and hope that it can reach, my friends and the stranger,

I found something better, weeks after I left my old weight behind,
a place where I was welcomed, by the honest and the kind,

While my life was not perfect, and other issues persist,
the weight that almost crushed me, is now on my past list,

I hope this inspires you, to take a chance at something greater,
than a life of misery, that turns a person into a hater,

Even if that isn't you, and you are reading this for other reasons,
I hope you remember this, it may help others in their dark seasons,

Even if that doesn't happen, and you never encounter that strife,
thank you my friend for reading, and helping me choose life.

REAPER

A man who was wealthy, millions to spare,
walked into the doctor's office, without a single care,

Until the doctor saw something strange, "I'm sending you for another test,"
leaving him to ponder, *how long until I'm laid to rest,*

He didn't want to die, he was only 64,
He could have additional decades, maybe a century more,

He grew more desperate, as the treatments began to fail,
his health deteriorated, as he became pale,

Finally in his crisis, he screamed to be spared,
all must have heard him, except the hearing impaired,

Finally the reaper came, faceless and cloaked in black,
the dying man was so scared, he almost had a heart attack,

The reaper spoke, with a dark ominous voice,
offering this dying man, a rare offer, a choice,

The man offered him money, but the reaper didn't budge,
he offered the reaper a yacht, this didn't move him a nudge,

Finally the reaper asked, "What will you do to keep your life,
will you do anything, even cut off your hand with a knife?"

The man said, "I will do anything, what do you want, name its worth,"
the reaper responded, "You must do the worst job on earth,"

"For how long?" The man asked as his neck did bend,
"Until you can do it no longer, until the very end,"

The man signed his name, on the dotted line,
he then asked "What job is it?" the Reaper responded, "Mine,"

The Reaper took the man's hand, as everything transferred through,
now the old reaper was gone, all that was left was the new,

He now had the power, to take those who were gone,
he was now the enemy, just a terrible pawn,

He never saw his family and friends, or his vast wealth,
the only good side of this whole thing, was the return of his health,

He moved at lightning speed, to every one of the dead,
it felt like a few days, but it was four minutes instead,

The hardest part of it all, taking people from their crying loved ones,
he couldn't stand their agonized stills, his guilt weighed ten tonnes,

It felt like weeks, but it had been an hour,
all the guilt, was no longer worth the power,

He finally found a man, after his own heart,
who was prepared to cut a deal, another one who thought he was smart,

So the new reaper, made the deal as the old one had,
the man thought he won the lottery, boy would he be mad,

The deal was made, as the dotted line was signed,
and relief came across his face, peace he would finally find,

As the newest reaper now wore the cloak, and regained feeling in his socket,
he found a piece of paper, written in his pocket,

It said, "Whoever took the deal, one of my desperate brothers,
when one will do anything for immortality, it guarantees the death of others."

WALLS OF BLOOD

The police came to the scene, to an apartment of death,
they'd seen bad things before, but this stole their breath,

His plain white walls were painted in his blood, dark red,
he laid there apparently collapsed, it looked like gallons he had bled,

The investigation began, no sign of foul play,
it looked like suicide, done an unusual way,

It wasn't a bullet to the head, or the slitting of a wrist,
it was cuts on his hands, rarely if ever on the list,

As they searched the apartment, they found the note on his bed,
they reluctantly wanted to know, what was in his head,

His name was Jake, he had contracted HIV,
the last few months had been hell, worse than what he could foresee,

His family kept their distance, his friends abandoned him,
as if he was poison, scared even to touch a limb,

He had to keep it a secret, he became a source of fear,
they had forgotten, it was a man standing here,

No one wanted him anymore, he felt like his blood was acid,
nothing makes you feel lower, nothing leaves you more flaccid,

The situation seemed hopeless, he was going to raise the white flag,
but as he did, he would leave his mark and tag,

He would show them the blood wasn't acid,
he would show them what it could do,
the note ended asking, "What does my painting look like to you?"

They saw it differently now, something beautiful out of something hideous,
however there was still sadness, and something insidious,

What a shame he resorted to this, others could have extended their hands,
counsellors, psychiatrists, and other brands,

There was also a story in the paper, of infants being cured,
perhaps he too could have been, if he had endured,

However the hardest part of all, another casualty of another fight,
is that in the battle against discrimination, there is no end in sight.

THE TRIA*N*GLE

As you wake up, in this world of ours,
the issue at hand, takes years not hours,

You are at one point, with two others across the land,
one landing in fantasy, and the other in reality's hand,

All three points move, for various reasons,
shifting closer and further away, during the different seasons,

What are these other two points, which we are negotiating between,
the battle that occurs, in every child and teen,

The adults must face it too, and risk falling short,
of the challenge of balance, through which we must sort,

The three points I speak of, can be separated by the sea,
who you are, you want to be and who you need to be,

Who you are will shift a lot, as you learn and age,
as will your dreams, as you continue to read the page,

In your dreams you may be famous, the rock star with it all,
no problems to deal with, just a groupie named Doll,

Who you need to be, the most constructive use of your skills,
maybe it's an accountant, who knows how to manage the bills,

Other forks in the road lay before you, what sort of person will you be,
will you be warm and generous, or the selfish me, me, me,

Perhaps your choice is hard, you wish you could avoid the situation,
of having to tell someone you love to stop, you dread the confrontation,

As you get closer in life, to the choices that will define you,
here is something to think about, consider the philosophy as new,

Some will tell you to drop your ideal, the responsible road is clear,
some will tell you to chase your dream, only a failure gives in to fear,

Once you know, where the other two points are,
try to bring them together, you may surprise the doubters with how far,

You reach and how sustainable, your path has become,
and how far you have moved, from the point you have come from,

The triangle is there for everyone, it can be conquered although a rarity,
when all three points have merged, and become a fulfilled singularity.

ROBOT'S REALIZATION

The scientists were gathered around, their creation ready to be awoke,
as they reminisced about their work, and how their lab almost went broke,

They flipped the switch, as the data was loaded,
all those tasks and information, took forever to get coded,

Finally the eyes turned on, as the robot examined what it saw,
the gears began to turn, as it opened its jaw,

And asked if all could hear it, the doctor nodded her head,
it began to rise, out of its unusual bed,

They began to ask it questions, from a data sample,
they couldn't ask it all, its knowledge was too ample,

As it passed test after test, one engineer's family came in from the rain,
the little boy asked "How do you feel," it responded "I don't feel any pain,"

One of the psychologists was puzzled, that answer seemed out of place,
so tomorrow he asked the same question, looking right in its face,

Just like before, it said exactly the same,
the robot responded, "I don't feel any pain,"

So they decided an interview was needed, why is it talking in this vein,
so they asked it once more, and it said "I don't feel any pain,"

They asked why that was its answer, the question of the session,
it responded, "Because that's what matters, it is the catalyst and obsession,

Some are obsessed with curing it, and will go to extremes,
some will hide from their senses, by drugging their way to dreams,

Some wish to cause it in others, schauden freude a negative joy,
some wish to embrace it, because it makes endorphins deploy,

That is your language, and the way you react,
sad pictures, hit harder than facts,

So I don't feel any pain, I am faring better than most,
but perhaps I made a mistake, and it came across as a boast,"

The psychologist spoke up, "There is more to life than that,
fulfilling potential and dreams, you are living proof of that,"

The robot responded, "You are an exception, an atypical joint,
mass behavioural data, proves a different point,

Even if you are correct, and there is fulfillment to be embraced and warmed,
why is it that so many, remain so uninformed?"

ART BECOMING SCIENCE

What was the magic, of that musical note,
what was the passion, in the poem that was wrote,

Why is that painting, more than an image,
or the sculpture, more than just a visage,

We didn't know, it was just a mystery,
something wonderful from, a less than pleasant history,

Words sometimes give away, more than was intended,
and examination could get, our current view suspended,

What words are used, to describe music and movies today,
generic, formulaic, not original in any way,

Notice the word formulaic, a formula, an equation,
this plus this and that, equals that situation,

The formula of the movies, that appeal to our psychology,
are being mapped and standardized, plus help from computer technology,

So are we reaching the day, when all music will be the same,
because they think it is perfect now, no need to change the game,

That hits certain notes, dictated by the equation,
that is designed to appeal to everyone, loved in every nation,

Do not be afraid, if you fear this is to come,
because we do not march, to the beat of just one drum,

We are individuals, we are not a computer or clone,
we have desires and dreams, that are purely our own,

There will always be those, that want something more,
something different and more interesting, or deeper to the core,

So is art becoming science, yes to a degree,
to some it is a formula, just repeat and agree,

Many of us step forward, as individual minds,
ready to appeal to others, with interests of similar kinds,

What stands out is what is different, so one will stand apart,
if it is done right, it will reach our mind and heart,

Finally we say, our voices shall be heard,
we will not be censored, our language will not be blurred,

We are individuals, let's keep looking for another way,
in the end it will be the strange, who swoop in and save the day.

WHISPERS IN THE FOREST

Did you hear them, do you know what they're doing,
she saw them together, I think they're screwing,

Did you hear about her, she loves the bottle,
did you hear about the ticket, he really hit the throttle,

Did you hear they're divorcing, who do you think is at fault,
he dresses weird, I think it's a cult,

If these sound familiar, they are the whispers from behind trees,
said by gossipers, don't tell them please,

Some know it is wrong, but are also to blame,
attracted to it, like a moth to a flame,

Here are the questions, that will determine if you are,
would you say it to their face, if they were more near than far,

Also when you talk, do you have any concern,
or do you enjoy their misfortune, or scandalous turn,

Some may try to stop, and to them I say thanks,
there are better things to do, than to reduce other's ranks,

However if you refuse to change, it's something for everyone to do,
then how would you feel, if the whispers in the forest surrounded you?

COMPLETELY BACKWARDS

Have you seen those videos, why I'm a feminist in the title,
let me tell you why some are not, with details so vital,

It started out well enough, demanding the right to vote,
wanting to be heard as equals, not as a child's note,

It has progressed to the workplace, equal pay for equal work,
who could be against that, some misogynist jerk,

The movement became so big, like most movements do,
but certain segments of it, became reprehensible through and through,

They stopped being about choice, and opening society's doors,
to being nagging and complaining, about the small issues of yours,

Don't play video games, movies don't pass our test,
women can't be portrayed wrong, but we won't tell you the best,

How dare women show off their body, the sisterhood is unimpressed,
once again no reason or guidelines, of how they should be dressed,

We may be used to it now, but imagine how this looks elsewhere,
where women still are second class citizens, for what issues do they care,

They stand defiant naked, proud not ashamed,
they are standing up for themselves, at the risk of being maimed,

We should be demanding more choice, not less miss or mister,
it's still a controlling force, whether they are big brother or big sister,

So what would I call myself, in this world of classification,
well for now I like egalitarian, a small but growing nation,

I stand for equality, men have problems too,
a lot of debating left, of issues old and new,

So I say to the feminists, who are embracing a radical path,
look at how you've deviated, from the original goals and hath,

Become the new shamers, how dare they show everything,
giving men ideas, old beliefs that aren't changing,

So I am an egalitarian, let's have rights for all,
I hope my group doesn't become backwards, and endure a similar fall.

IN A TAVERN

Knowledge speaks but wisdom listens, Jimmy Hendrix was so right,
what will the bartender learn, as she listens tonight,

The usual things happen, watching hockey and football,
cheering for the big plays, attacking the referee's bad call,

But tonight she looks around, hearing the conversations,
all the negativity, the opposite of celebrations,

She turns her ear to one table, of four injured souls,
yet their conversation, has an odd goal,

"I got injured the worst, I lost a hand,"
"Well I lost the lower half of my leg," what a tragic band,

Another says "My lungs were damaged, don't you see the oxygen tank there,"
the other said "I'm a paraplegic, so I'm stuck in this wheelchair,"

The bartender shook her head, as her apron began to chafe,
wondering "Why aren't they asking, why their workplaces are so unsafe,"

She looked at another table, where two women began to bicker,
they were getting upset, as their tempers began to flicker,

"Don't you know what I've been through, my husband beat me up,
I was scared to death, afraid to drink from the wrong cup,

It got so bad, my ribs were broken and had to be taped"
the other said "You think that's bad, I was molested as a child; repeatedly raped,"

They tried to justify why they each had it worse, and the other's pain was less,
the bartender thought, "Bad parenting and misogyny caused their mess,"

Why are they discussing their trauma, in this odd way?
she turned to another table, a question for another day,

This table had two men, one was gay and the other was black,
their conversation heated as well, their passion having no lack,

"Gays weren't slaves, the black people really got screwed"
the gay man said "For millenniums we were killed, washed out of history dude,"

He responded "Slavery was worse than death, besides have you seen the news?
Police brutality, how many lives do we have to lose?"

The bartender needed a minute, to absorb all she had heard,
she took a second look at those tables, with her vision clear and un-blurred,

All had been victims, of the cruelty of others,
but were forgetting they weren't alone, sitting next to their sisters and brothers,

There is no way, to deny the reality of their pain,
yet there is one more tragedy, making their appeals in vain,

Regardless of their background, or whether they are saints or sinners,
in a suffering contest, there truly are no winners.

WALK A MILE

One night I was watching TV, another night hanging out with the guys,
when I saw an ad, that took me by surprise,

They were showing homeless people, reading mean things that were tweeted,
it brought them to tears, how these words were treated,

My friend pulled up his tablet, and followed the link,
to see what had been written, how the tweeters think,

The tweets were harsh and cold, malice woven throughout,
did they even know, what they were talking about,

I doubt they even know, how people become homeless in the first place,
the tweeters never looked at reality, with an honest face,

Some of the homeless have problems with drugs,
as if the tweeters don't have a vice,
some have mental illnesses, that's no excuse to be colder than ice,

Some parents abandoned them, due to intolerance or neglect,
that is not the children's fault, take pause and reflect,

Many simply fell through the cracks, opportunity is hard to find,
I guess it's harder to be informed, than it is to be unkind,

I am not an expert, but it's a path that no one would choose,
if you think otherwise, try walking a mile in their shoes.

BUNNY HEAVEN

A pet is like family, they become part of your life,
until the day comes, like being stabbed by a knife,

You have to put them down, you have to let them go,
they may be sick or injured, what to do, you know,

That time came to me, one day in June,
as we reluctantly agreed, this would be Luffy's last moon,

As the injection went in, and she drifted into space,
it was heart wrenching, as tears flowed down my face,

At that moment, of great pain for the family Howe,
the veterinarian with great empathy, said "She's in bunny heaven now",

The brief image in my head, of rabbits here and there,
was comforting and adorable, but it was an illusion, not fair,

We have no reason, to believe in such a place,
no matter if it brings, a smile to a face,

Even those that believe in heaven, wouldn't defend the notion,
and would try to change the subject, because questions would be in motion,

Why do people talk about heaven, for animals at all,
it's another fairy tale, giving a clue to the one so tall,

Death is unpleasant, some can't handle loss,
some fear being under the tombstone, forgotten covered with moss,

What a wonderful idea, there's a place that is perfection,
call it whatever, as long as people can follow direction,

When you consider when these ideas were born, a life in need of escape,
most people dying in their 40's, here comes another gang ready to rape,

You could die at any time, safety was a fantasy's joke,
people so impoverished and desperate, they wish for what we call broke,

That life would be a nightmare, begging for hope in any frame,
it should be no surprise, a good afterlife goes by many names,

Heaven, Paradise, Valhalla, don't forget the Elysian field,
places where all is perfect, your fate is not sealed,

Now we can see through it, we have learned to grieve,
here is the realization, many have yet to receive,

The day will come, when we draw our last breath,
only one thing is undefeated, we call it death,

The memories we leave behind, may get blown away by the breeze,
even if we have statues, ask for a century please,

In time all of us will fade, but that's not admitting defeat,
If we're lucky we get a turn, to experience the passionate heat,

Of living a joyful life, with people you embrace and love,
being happy with what you did here, not waiting for what's above,

My pet rabbit is gone, I faced and dealt with that pain,
I know for sure, I will never see her again,

But I accept that the day we fade is coming, we can only run so fast,
if you helped bring heaven here, you have earned your peace at last.

MORE

He has the eye of the tiger, float like a butterfly, sting like a bee,
he's smart as a fox, or maybe a chimpanzee,

Fast as a cheetah, ruthless as a shark,
he took apart the old guy, the dinosaur in the park,

If these sound familiar, what do they really say,
how these are said without question, day after day,

Other things are said too; they're lean, they're mean,
they are an insert task here machine,

What an odd statement, why am I making a fuss,
I have to wonder, how animals would assign traits to us,

What a mixed bag that would be, take a moment and pause,
also wonder why you would remain human, and the reasons because,

Even if you were given a choice, how few would trade it all,
despite all the traits listed above, more and more to call,

So why do we assign such traits, and rarely say "like a human being"
the answer stares us in the face, read on you will be seeing,

Perhaps why we add animal descriptions
and buy those products on the shelves
is because unfortunately, we always want
to be more than ourselves.

THE RAVEN'S ARRIVAL

As I wander weak and weary, to my home tired and teary,
not sure if I am seeing clearly,

All the lights refuse to turn on
all but the darkness is gone,

As I mourn the passing, of the one in a photograph,
so happy and joyful at one time, now struggling for a laugh,

As the door knocks, I approach peering out the window,
I see nothing but I open up and in it flows,

On the air currents of despair, breaching my only haven,
it flies upstairs, the shadow, the raven,

I run upstairs after it, but it remains out of reach,
I follow into my room, and begin my speech,

"Get out, get out, fly out my bedroom door,"
it stands on top of my mirror, quote the Raven, "Nevermore"

It casts a shadow across the room, engulfing who I see in the mirror,
it is too much to bear, I speak up with a tear,

"Let it be, let it be, why must you haunt me,
why can't you just leave the past, and out of where I can see?

Leave behind no feather, just leave and make no returns,
your gaze is hell, a look that strikes and burns,"

As it stood there stoic, "You will fly out my bedroom door,"
the Raven gripped the mirror stronger, quote the Raven, "Nevermore"

As I look in the mirror, the shadow so deeply cast,
like a room flooded in black, painted by the past,

I find a smaller mirror, sitting on my nightstand,
I look in it and see the Raven, smaller than my hand,

I see the spark in my eye, duller but brighter than low,
the spark in the eye of the child, in that old photo,

I turn around defiantly, through a tidal wave of shadow,
despite the terror inflicted, by this bird that would not go,

I tell it "I will not run, my spark is still in me,
I will fight until anyone, anywhere can see,

I will smile again," quote the Raven "Nevermore,"
I replied "I will fight until you leave, and if not Forevermore."

Stories

LEGENDARY SECRET AGENT

One day Gordon and Clevon were having lunch and they were excited to meet Alvin Levitt; he was the most legendary agent that the agency had ever had, it seemed like he was immortal, nothing could kill him, nothing was more than he could handle. The joke around the office was that Alvin Levitt could play James Bond and the only acting he would have to do would be the British accent. The stories about him became so great, it became hard to separate the man from the legend.

Gordon and Clevon began talking about him, Gordon started, "Legend has it that he was once thrown out of a plane from 800 yards in the air, he took off his jacket and used it as a parachute to land safely on the ground."

Clevon and Gordon chuckled when Clevon said, "Yeah, that's a good one, but one of the best stories I ever heard was that he was on a submarine that was a mile deep in the ocean and it had been attacked and was leaking. I heard that in just a few minutes, he sank the enemy sub then he figured out how to maneuver the sub so that he could blast it back to surface before the air ran out."

Gordon responded, "That's great but then I heard about this story: he had tracked down a weapons dealer in Antarctica and things went south, they caught him except he escaped, blew the place up and walked for 22 straight hours in the freezing cold to the nearest settlement. Right after he got there they put some warm blankets on him and he asks for some ice, they look at him like he's crazy. They ask him 'You almost froze to death, why would you want ice?' He looks at them 'Because the thought of a martini with ice is what kept me going all this time.'"

They both chuckled hysterically and were simultaneously amazed by what this incredible man had done, Clevon insisted on telling one more story that he had heard. "Supposedly a spy had been sent to intercept him and lure him into a trap. She was this hot chick – Playboy playmate material – and just when her group thought they had him everybody came in and surrounded the place. Her and half a dozen others surrendered and they ask him 'How did you know?' and he responded 'She talks in her sleep'."

They laughed and laughed, revelling in the legend of this person they admired so much, their excitement of his arrival was building to a crescendo. Within a few minutes of this conversation Alvin Levitt came through the door to a standing ovation as he waved to all of them. He looked exactly as they expected, a fine suit, not a hair out of place, a confident smile and very handsome. He was there to give a motivational speech about the importance of their work. His most noteworthy statement was, "Keeping the world safe will never be an easy job, but if we are prepared to walk to the ends of the Earth or fight our enemy at the bottom of the ocean, we can keep the way of life that our people need and deserve." With that he waved and walked off to a standing ovation from the crowd overcome with admiration.

Alvin had gone upstairs after the talk however he was in the elevator when Gordon and Clevon were coming into it. The instant the doors closed they couldn't resist asking questions about this legend standing in their presence. At first Alvin tried to sweep the questions under the rug until the elevator jolted and they realized they were stuck.

Now Alvin knew he was trapped and as their questions began to barrage him, he finally lost his temper, "Would you shut up, those stories are exaggerations at best and fairy tales at worst."

Clevon with his jaw trembling asked, "Wait you didn't use your jacket as a parachute from 800 yards in the air?"

He looked at them in disbelief, "No you idiot, I took off my jacket so I could use the parachute that I had underneath."

Gordon asked him, "What about the 22 hours in the arctic, didn't you come in and ask for a martini on the rocks?"

He said, "No I've never been south of Paraguay or north of Calgary."

Clevon then asked, "What about the submarine?"

Alvin responded, "It was 100 feet underwater, not a mile. People exaggerate so damn much."

Gordon said, "What about the hot spy chick, you figured out what she was doing when you heard her talking in her sleep?"

He rolled his eyes, "I knew she was a spy the whole damn time, we never slept together and I put that line out there as wit, it was nothing more. She also wasn't the perfect ten that everyone talks about either."

Gordon and Clevon looked at each other and asked him, "Wait then how come you told everyone that you accomplished your legendary feats because of your passion and commitment?"

He said, "Look, we need the most loyal people we can get, and if we have to augment the truth to get them to perform they will pay me to do exactly that. The only problem is I'm tired of people thinking I'm James Bond for God's sake."

He took a deep breath and told them that for the good of the agency not to reveal anything of what they just heard. Gordon and Clevon's disappointment shone through as they began the very typical small talk one would expect while waiting for an elevator to start working.

Clevon went home that night really let down and heartbroken, he felt like such a fool for believing all of that stuff. When he finally got home he spoke to his wife about the usual things for a few minutes, as she prepared dinner he went into the living room and he watched his 4-year-old son playing with his new action figure.

As his son rushed to meet him and began talking a mile a minute about everything this superhero could do, "He can fly, he moves super-fast! When he's around criminals come in last."

He stared for a moment and saw the parallel, between his son and himself and saw the complete and udder belief in his child's eyes about this character's existence. If he told his son that his hero didn't exist he would have been just as heartbroken as he was. He told his son to wash up for dinner as he sat in his recliner and pondered, just as his wife said, "Dinner's ready," and he approached the table. He felt unfit in his shoes, he was the father of his house, he was a 36-year-old man and he began to wonder as he picked up his fork, "How much do we truly grow up?"

ONE MORE WISH

His name was Robert Selko, and he was a man who wanted more than anything to be rich and have things that would impress people. That became his life's goal, collecting rare and valuable things. Since he wasn't rich he took full advantage of minimum payments, all of his treasures were on credit.

One fateful day he was in an antique shop, and found a box that was locked, the lock looked like it had been there for centuries and was slowly rusting off. But what caught his eye wasn't the lock, but what was on top. The inscription appeared to be in Gaelic, "This is centuries old," he thought. He drove home with yet another item to add to his collection.

After reaching a stop light the lock on the box began to make him wonder. His curiosity overwhelmed him, he spent the rest of the evening trying to break the lock any way he could. Finally he had the lock barely hanging on, until he wrenched the lock as hard as he could and not only did the lock come off but the box fell off the table and hit the floor. There protruding out of the box was a spout, he opened the box the rest of the way, and saw it was a Genie's lamp.

At first he was dismissive thinking, "Genies are make believe, nothing is in here." However, he rubbed it anyway, he just couldn't resist the thought. Suddenly the lamp shook as purple smoke poured out and filled up the few feet around the lamp, emerging from the smoke was a pale white, red bearded man wearing bright blue and green.

"Oh my God," Robert blurted out.

The Genie looked around as he began to stretch his limbs as the smoke dissipated, he saw Robert was the only man around, and the only one that could have awakened him. He was only briefly puzzled by his surroundings.

"I am the Genie of the lamp," the Genie said with authority. "You are the one who awakened me and therefore you will receive 70 wishes."

Robert's jaw hung from his face in astonishment. He asked, "Wait a minute, you, are telling me, that you are a Genie that grants wishes? To top it off, not only am I getting three wishes, I'm getting 70?"

The Genie responded, "Yes, however, there are two rules: first, you must say what you wish for and start by saying 'I wish'. The second is that you cannot wish for more wishes."

Robert was almost orgasmic and ready to celebrate, "With 70 wishes, why would I need more?"

He began to ponder the possibilities of everything he could have. Then he realized he could quit his job, he could wake up and go to bed whenever he wanted, go wherever he wanted and his life could become the ultimate party and vacation. So he was ready.

"Genie, I wish for $1 trillion in cash."

The Genie nodded, as the room overflowed with cash, so much that Robert was lost in it. Robert barely managed to yell, "I wish to be saved!" The Genie rescued him teleporting him to the top of the stairs, as Robert became angry. "Why did you almost drown me?"

The Genie responded, "You wished for $1 trillion in cash, as you can see it takes up a lot of space."

Robert looked from upstairs seeing an ocean of money. "Be more careful next time," Robert bickered.

The Genie said, "You are the wisher, you must be careful with your next 68 wishes."

He then responded, "Okay Genie, I wish for you to hide all of this money in the basement, closet and the spare guest room."

The Genie agreed and said, "It is done. You have 67 wishes left."

Robert was annoyed that it took three wishes to get the money and store it conveniently, but at least he had plenty of wishes left.

The next day he decided that he was going to tell off the CEO of his company. When Robert arrived at work, he went into the washroom, rubbed the lamp and made his wish.

"Genie I wish for a loud 30-man marching band with 'I quit Tago' written on their jackets and their instruments to accompany me to the CEO's office and back out of the office, and for no one to stop us."

The Genie replied and told him, "The marching band will arrive ten seconds after you leave this room."

Robert had some status in the company, but Mr. Tago the CEO, had disregarded Robert at nearly every turn. Finally, he stepped out of the washroom, with the lamp in his briefcase and the marching band came around the corner ten seconds later as planned. They marched through the office to the astonishment of everyone.

Mr. Tago came out of his office upset, "What the hell is going on here?"

He saw Robert leading the marching band, then the band grew silent, as Robert said, "I have waited four years to tell you this: you are a cranky old asshole, and kiss my ass because I don't have to work for you anymore." He proudly marched away leading the band out of the building. Robert's smile became a mile wide, he had waited four years for this moment, and he was relishing every second.

After he got home he checked his social media links and saw that everyone was wondering what was going on. The most common sentiments were "Did he go crazy?" as well as "Did he win the lottery?"

He immediately checked his e-mail and realized that not only were people asking what happened, they were asking for money. He knew that once he started handing out money, they would never stop bothering him. He quickly called on the Genie and said, "I wish for no one to ask me for loans or free money. That should stop the moochers." The Genie accepted this and reminded him there was 65 left.

Now that he had solved that problem, it was time to party.

He said, "Genie, I wish for an invite to the next party at the Playboy Mansion." The Genie granted it and reminded him that he had 64 wishes left.

As he looked at the invitation Robert saw that it wasn't for another two weeks; for tonight he searched the Internet for the hottest club in the city. He was going to paint the town red with all his money; he went on a shopping spree that afternoon for the most stylish clothes in the mall; he rented a limousine and just as the clock struck 8, he realized that there was one thing missing: he needed to be a great dancer. He wished for the Genie to make him a master of all dancing styles. The Genie accepted this and reminded him that 63 wishes remained.

He went to the club, he left the lamp in the limousine, he walked in and bought drinks for everyone who was at the bar, and was having the night of his life. He was partying more than he had in years, it was all great. He found one woman and began to charm her, impressed by his incredible dancing skills. She took pictures of them together, he took her back to his hotel. They had sex, he was thrilled by his new conquest and afterwards she went home. Right after this, he was going back to the club.

He thought to himself, "Why not do it again? Just have a couple energy drinks, I'm not that tired."

After he went back to the club, he was attacked. He was punched in the face as the crowd gasped, the attacker proceeded to yell, "You screwed my wife!"

Robert had no idea, he didn't see a ring and she had said nothing about anyone else in her life. Now her jealous husband was ready to kill him. Robert ran through the club to the men's room, and hid around the corner as he went in the room. Just five or six seconds later, the attacker ran in, as Robert quietly but quickly went out the door. He immediately ran to his limo, telling the limo driver to drive as fast as he could. The limousine sped away with Robert looking out the back window relieved that it looked like he had lost his attacker.

After Robert got home he summoned the Genie, and the Genie asked, "Have you decided on your next wish?"

Robert responded, "Yes, I wish for no one besides us to remember anything I did from 8 pm until right now."

The Genie granted it, all of a sudden Robert remembered that there were still pictures. "Genie," he said, "I wish for any pictures or video copies, digital or physical of me taken since 8 pm to be removed from existence." The Genie granted this as well and reminded him that he had 61 left. He took a deep breath for the bullet he had dodged and now if he ever ran into that man again he would have nothing to worry about.

The Playboy party still wasn't for another two weeks and he decided he needed a vacation, especially after the stressful close call from the night before. He bought his tickets, so he could visit Europe for ten days. The plane left the next night, his passport was set, he had his money ready and he was going to cross another item off his bucket list.

The next day as he was looking up things to see in England, Scotland and Ireland, he suddenly realized one problem; getting the lamp past the metal detectors at the airport. If the lamp was detected and discovered, it could cost him the Genie and the remaining wishes. He decided to call on the Genie again, "I wish for you to make the lamp undetectable to metal detectors, x-rays and anything else that could scan the inside of my luggage."

The Genie granted it and said, "You have 60 wishes left."

Robert rolled his eyes being tired of the frequent updates. After a pause he responded, "Genie, I wish for you to stop giving me updates of how many wishes I have left."

The Genie shook his head in disappointment as the wish was granted and Robert had 59 left.

Robert went to London first as he saw all the sights, his first night he went to an expensive club in London, just outside of the city core, in a rented limo. Remembering what had happened before, he wished for the Genie to place a green light over the heads of any single girls in the club that only Robert could see. It was done and Robert was delighted that he didn't have to worry about what happened last time or that he didn't have to be reminded how many wishes he had left.

The plan went off perfectly, he took his masterful dancing skills with his money and charm, and had women throwing themselves at him. However, all of that green light became annoying, so just before one girl got into his limo, he asked her to wait outside of it for one moment. Robert called the Genie out of his lamp, he wished for the Genie to turn the green lights off. The Genie shook his head, because he was the only one that knew or cared that Robert had 57 wishes left, all he seemed to care about was his next conquest.

As the night went on in his hotel room, Robert was having the time of his life. However, as she began to ask him personal things like "What do you do for a living?" and "Do you have any other women in your life?" He realized he needed to lose her quick. He might have a hard time with other conquests if she started stalking him. Robert asked her to get him a snack from the lobby.

The instant she left, he asked, "Genie, I wish for her to leave the hotel, and decide that a one night stand is good enough."

The Genie granted it, as Robert began to ponder the rest of his vacation. As they went through Scotland, a thunderstorm was coming, so Robert asked, "Genie, I wish for you to stop this thunderstorm from happening, and for the weather to be nothing but sunny the entire time I am here."

Instantly the clouds began to dissipate, and the sun began to shine through, Robert had a nice few days. Before he left, he found out that there was a caber toss tournament going on, with a prize of 5000 British pounds and a trophy. While he had all the money he could want, Robert couldn't resist the trophy and the glory of the crowd, so he called on the Genie again.

"Genie, I wish to be the best caber toss athlete in all of Scotland today." The Genie granted his wish, keeping his disappointment to himself. As Robert celebrated the victory to the applause of hundreds, the Genie shook his head whispering to himself, "54 left."

It was only nine days until the party at the Playboy Mansion, and Robert was heading to Ireland. After arriving in Ireland, Robert saw a few sights and then went out into the country to see the rolling green hills. He called the Genie out, and said, "Welcome home."

Although it had changed over the centuries, there was still that familiarity in the rural area overlooking the green rolling hills. The Genie began to tear up as he muttered, "You damn fool."

Robert became angry, "What the hell, I show you your homeland and you're insulting me, get back in the lamp."

The Genie tried to tell him, "I wasn't talking about you," but Robert snapped back, "Don't lie to me, now get back in there, now!" The Genie returned to the lamp as Robert prepared to go visit the Irish pubs and party all night.

After a night of drinking and partying, the limousine driver and two others helped him back to his hotel room. Shortly after being left there, Robert realized he was about to be sick. He called the Genie again, "Genie, I wish for my stomach to calm down and not throw up." The Genie granted it, and then shortly before passing out, Robert said, "I wish to not have a hangover in the morning." The Genie granted it as Robert was passed out on his bed.

The next morning Robert woke up feeling good but barely remembering anything, he suddenly became worried and called on the Genie. "Genie, I wish for you to tell me what happened last night, wait, show me on the TV." The Genie put the footage on the TV, Robert saw himself dancing and drinking. Then he saw himself almost passed out being carried by the limousine driver and a few other people. He was relieved that they didn't steal anything.

The video ended with Robert making his previous two wishes before passing out. The Genie asked Robert if there was anything else he wanted. Robert responded, "Yes, I wish for my body to be able to handle any amount of drinking without negative health effects, without throwing up or hangovers the next morning." The Genie granted this and Robert said he was going for breakfast and would be going somewhere else in the afternoon. The Genie was the only one that was keeping track that he had already used up 20 of his wishes and that 50 wishes remained.

By this point in the trip, Robert had done his fair share of shopping for old junk, and kept ordering new things to be shipped back home. So after coming home he had all of these things dropped off in his garage. He didn't want them to go inside his house because after all, he didn't want them to see the piles of money lying around.

He now had just a few days left until the Playboy party; he decided that he would rest up for two days before flying out there. He realized that while he was gone the rumours about him had spread like wildfire. Even though no one was asking him for money they were posting a lot of rumours on his Facebook page.

Now his mother was worried and she had called eight times from her home in Florida and even said that she was on her way up, and would be there tomorrow. He called her immediately, and tried to talk her out of it, but she wouldn't let up, she was scared that he had gotten involved in organized crime, or something else that was dangerous. Robert felt like his mother was over-bearing, which is why he was so happy when she moved to Florida two years earlier.

He immediately called the Genie, "Genie, first I wish for my mother's flight to be cancelled, refunded and for her to decide she doesn't have to visit or call me at all." The Genie granted this, and then Robert said, "Genie, I also wish for my mother and any other friends, family or other people to stop worrying about me." The Genie granted it, Robert then made one more wish. "Genie, I wish for no one else to spread any more rumours about me from now on."

The Genie granted it, Robert then tried to figure out what else he could do to maximize his experience at the Playboy Mansion. He then said, "Genie, I wish for the perfect tan and for it to go away on its own as a normal tan would." The Genie granted this and as he looked in the mirror and admired how good he looked, the Genie thought that he should be looking at the 46 wishes that remained.

During his two resting days, he was trying to figure out where to put everything and he began to realize that his house was too small, so he decided he was going to upgrade. He began looking for new homes and also began wondering about where else he could live now that he was unbelievably wealthy. He eventually discovered a very wealthy neighbourhood in South Carolina with big multi-million dollar homes. His eyes lit up as he considered what he could do now, his imagination ran wild, he could have parties and show people all of his exotic things and people would finally admire them rather than wondering why he collected junk. His home could become his own personal museum. So he made a phone call to the real estate agents there to begin looking for a new mansion.

He still was getting ready to go to the Playboy Mansion Party, once he arrived he began to realize that there weren't very many people interested in talking to him. Everyone was either talking to the celebrities, or the Bunnies, but he was getting lost in the shuffle. As wonderful as the surroundings were, it wasn't as much fun as he thought it would be. Then they announced that there was going to be a dance contest at nine o'clock. He knew that this would be his chance to win everyone over and suddenly he would get the attention he was craving.

Unfortunately, before the dance contest could begin one of the organizers spotted him and asked him who he was.

He responded, "Robert Selko," and so she asked to see his invitation. He showed it to her, it looked exactly like all the other invitations.

She said, "Thank you, have a great night."

He was relieved thinking that the concern had passed; what he didn't realize was that she knew something didn't make sense, she asked around and no one knew who he was or why he was invited. This was when she called security to detain him, she suspected that he had hacked their computers to get himself an invitation. After all, these parties were very exclusive and they were very careful about who was invited.

As Robert began to strike up a conversation, four men in suits told him to come with them immediately. He knew he was in trouble and asked "Why?"

The organizer responded, "How did you get invited to this party?"

Robert made up a quick lie, "Hef invited me."

She rolled her eyes and said, "Nice try but he's never seen you before in his life."

Robert knew that the lamp was in his rented car, which was parked at the front of the mansion, and if he got taken into custody he would risk losing the Genie. He decided to run for it, as security chased after him. He managed to hide behind one of the large carved shrubs, but within a few seconds he had to keep running because one of them spotted him, he realized that he had to get to his car no matter what. He saw his car in the distance, he ran with everything he had, he could make them forget, he could wipe out everything that had just happened, all he had to do was rub that lamp and make his wish.

He was just 20 feet away as the security guard grabbed him and he struggled to get away, he saw a loose brick in front of this row of parked cars and he bashed the security guard in the head with it as he kept running for his car. He immediately opened his car when he saw the other security guards coming and he said, "Genie I wish to wipe out the memories of everything that has happened in the last hour, and replace it with what it would be if Hef told that woman that I was his friend's cousin."

The Genie granted it and he suddenly found that he had fallen over, dazed from an entirely different hour of reality hitting him all at once. Everything was fine, and the dance contest was about to start, he was about to show these people his incredible skills.

As the dance contest began they started with salsa and he amazed people with his perfect technique, and his incredible skill in break dancing. Before he knew it, one of the most popular hit rappers, T.R.B. otherwise known as the Ticking Rhyme Bomb, asked him where he learned to dance like that. Robert just began to talk about how it came naturally to him, he thought he would start soaking in the praise, but this turned into something more. T.R.B. responded by saying that he wanted to do a music video that takes place in an underground dance contest and he wanted Robert to teach all the extras how to dance like him. It would pay very well and he promised lots of women for the after party. Robert said, "Sure," but there was one big problem: he didn't know how to do the moves – he had just wished and they had been granted.

As he looked over the party he had tried to hit on the various women only to discover that Miss April, Miss August and Miss November weren't interested in him. Even the server bunnies weren't allowed to fraternize with the guests, so he realized that as much as he was having fun, he needed a little bit of help. After getting T.R.B.'s phone number, Robert slipped away from the party, went back to his car, and he summoned the Genie.

"Genie, you did a wonderful job changing everything, tonight is going well, but I still need your help." The Genie asked him what his wishes were, and Robert responded, "I wish for Miss April, Miss August and Miss November to want to have sex with me tonight."

The Genie said, "Granted."

Robert continued, "I wish for them to want to share me." The Genie granted it.

Finally Robert said, "I wish to have the stamina and the skill to sexually satisfy them for hours."

He got out of his car, with the lamp in a bag, ready to have a night that most men only dream about, a night that no one would believe, but that he would remember forever. He suddenly stopped and realized that if they left the property something might be suspicious, and he didn't want to have to run from security again.

So he went back to his car and wished for the Genie to ensure that no one would interrupt his time with the three women and that they would be allowed to go to one of the mansion's bedrooms. As he went back to the party he immediately got the attention of all three of those Playmates and they went back to Miss August's room. After having a night of unbelievable sex, with them all seemingly having the time of their lives, eventually all of them fell asleep.

The next morning he woke up shortly before any of the women did, he had to take a few minutes to process everything that had happened and what officially didn't happen. He realized that he had come so close to losing the rest of his wishes, as well as potentially going to jail. He was so relieved that it didn't happen and he thought that next time he would have to be more careful. After he ate a great breakfast of chocolate chip pancakes he left the Playboy mansion knowing he would be invited back again for sure.

The rest of the morning Robert thought about the close call that almost cost him one of the greatest nights of his life. He needed to come up with a better plan, something that wouldn't leave him separated from his wishes.

Later that day he checked into a hotel room, he rubbed the lamp and summoned the Genie. When the Genie asked him what he wished for, Robert asked the Genie, "How close do you have to be to me in order to grant a wish?"

The Genie simply said, "I have to be able to hear it. I can only act on wishes that are told to me. If I can't hear them, I cannot grant them."

Robert said, "Okay, Genie I wish for you to dress in a modern suit and be within 20 feet of me at all times."

The Genie granted it, and Robert added, "From now on if anyone else asks, you are my assistant Mr. Genie… Lampshire."

The Genie accepted this with a resigned attitude and asked him what they were doing next. Robert decided that they would travel back from L. A. and figure out their next move. He suddenly realized an enormous problem, if the Genie was out of the lamp he would need to buy a ticket and he would have to go through airport security etc. So Robert took an enormous risk and said, "Genie, I wish for you to go back to my house and wait there for me."

The flight was a few hours for Robert to ponder how he was going to deal with the offer made by T.R.B. If he said no, he would be throwing away a golden opportunity, but he didn't even know how to dance – it had been granted to him – on top of that he didn't have patience to teach people. At his old job he didn't even like teaching the new people how to use the computer system, he thought to himself, "This is supposed to be a vacation and a party, not a new job. This isn't like my old job though, this is going to be something else entirely."

He got off the plane knowing exactly what his next wish would be, as he pulled up to his house, the Genie greeted him as he came through the front door. Robert said, "Genie, I wish for the ability to teach my dancing skill to others, so I will know how to do it and I can tell them." The Genie granted it, as Robert made the call to T.R.B.'s manager and said that he would be willing to teach his backup dancers and to let him know when they needed him so they could work out a time.

In the meantime he needed to figure out which new mansion he was going to buy. He looked at ones with pools, tennis courts even ones with bowling alleys, he was trying to figure out which features he wanted, he soon decided on one that was less than an hour's drive away from Myrtle Beach. That was where the big stuff was, he also decided that he would be able to take up and master golf. They apparently had a lot of nice golf courses down there and if he was going to be hanging out with and impressing rich people that would be a skill that he would need to know. So he called a lawyer to arrange the purchase of the house, he quickly realized his one big problem: How do you move almost $1 trillion in cash without anyone sneaking away with some of it? So he decided that he would sell his house after he bought the new one and he would wish his enormous pile of money over to it. Not yet, but soon.

He received a return phone call from T.R.B.'s manager who said that they would be filming the music video in three weeks and they wanted him to work 10 days with the backup dancers so they would know all the moves. He got all the information and booked the flight for himself and his assistant Genie Lampshire would be waiting at the airport.

He went out to do some grocery shopping and he was just picking up the box of Coke cans when he realized the Genie hadn't come with him, the Genie had to be within 20 feet of him at all times. After he came home, he asked the Genie what happened to that wish, The Genie responded that he himself broke the distance portion of the wish with the follow up wish that sent him back to Robert's house.

So Robert rolling his eyes said, "Fine, Genie I wish for you be invisible to everyone except me whenever we are travelling on planes or if I tell you to, and you must stay within 20 feet of me at all times. But if I tell you to go some-where and wait for me, as soon as we are reunited the rule comes back into effect until I tell you otherwise." The Genie granted it, as Robert blurted out, "I hate wasting wishes on technicality bullshit like that."

The Genie thought to himself, "You have wasted wishes already; you have used up almost half and now have 37 left."

Before he could leave to teach dance moves to the backup dancers Robert realized that he had not been paying attention to his bills as he got a letter stating that if he didn't pay his bill within 30 days they were going to repossess some of his items. He got irritated and he called the Genie again, "Genie, I wish for you to pay all my debts with some of my money." The Genie did this and now Robert was deciding on which mansion he was going to buy, he picked the one and he was set to move in the next month.

However he still had the issue of selling the current house, he decided to sell it as soon as he had access to the other one so he would be able to hide the money effectively. It then occurred to him that because he had not even spent the first million yet, and the mansion would cost $24 million he could find an easier way to store all this money. He wished for the Genie to take all the money and change it into $100 denominations in neat piles in the basement. The Genie agreed and while there were still piles and piles of money, the piles were not the overwhelming mess they had been.

Robert and the seemingly invisible Genie were flying to the studio where he would get to teach the backup dancers his moves. The knowledge was in his head, all he had to do was talk and he would look like a dancing expert.

As they flew, he saw a cute flight attendant and the temptation to join the mile high club was too great. The Genie was sitting in the seat to his right looking out the window.

Robert leaned over so he was right next to the Genie's ear. "Genie, I wish for her to invite me to have sex with her in the airplane bathroom in one minute."

The Genie granted it, and exactly one minute later she handed Robert a note that said, "I'm hot for you, meet me in the bathroom." He got up and as he went in excited for his newest conquest he had forgotten to lock the door. As everything progressed they were right in the middle of the deed when the door opened and a small child accompanied by their parent saw this in shock and began to yell and make a scene. Robert quickly pulled his pants up, as he ran out and wished the Genie to reverse everything that had happened in the last 15 minutes.

The Genie granted it, Robert in frustration took a deep breath. He was handed the same note by the flight attendant, saying she wanted him, he looked at the Genie and said, "I wish for no one to need to use the bathroom for the next hour and no one to look at the bathrooms for that hour." The Genie granted it as this time he went in and did the deed but could not enjoy it the same way he had before.

After they had finished, he went back to his seat and he overheard the supervising attendant asking the flight attendant where she had been, she had to make up a lie, but because of the hesitation the supervisor knew it and told her that he didn't believe her and that she was getting fired for this. She tried to ask the supervisor not to but it was no good, as Robert looked on conflicted, the Genie asked if he wanted to use a wish to help her. Robert turned around and said, "I have wasted too many wishes on technicalities, and she can deal with it."

The Genie stared out the window with disappointment, he had 32 wishes left but he wouldn't spare one for this woman who he had put into that situation. The Genie saw his faded reflection on the window, he could see his own disappointed look on his face, a look he knew only too well.

They got to the studio and within a couple of minutes T.R.B. introduced Robert, "Listen up dogs we got to shoot this video next week and I want it to come out crisp like a new C note. So this guy is going to be telling you all how to do the different routines, got it." Everyone nodded and he said, "Rob my boy, go to it." T.R.B. left as Robert knew that he had been told what he had to teach and he had already wished for the knowledge of how to teach.

Over the next two days he began to show the back-up dancers their moves as they learned quickly. However, he began to have problems with one of the main co-stars who was supposed to be the hero of the music video, the guy who was supposed to 'own the floor,' he thought that the moves were too quick. Robert began to grow impatient, as the second day ended he knew that he had to do this but he wasn't sure.

He asked the Genie for advice the Genie responded, "You just need patience and allow him to practice." Robert decided to keep patient, he had several more work days left before the actual shoot. Eventually everything began to come together and the video was shot and everything went off exactly as T.R.B. had hoped.

Later that night T.R.B. invited him to come for his after party, Robert had brought his assistant Genie Lampshire with him. During the party one of T.R.B.'s friends popped his head in the door, saying, "Hey boys, the strippers are here." Robert's eyes began to pop out of his head as these scantily clad beauties came in through the door.

As the drugs came out Robert noticed that T.R.B. was talking to someone who asked him, "Where did you get these from?"

As T.R.B. told him, the guy said, "Cool," and the other guy went into the bathroom. Robert began to get distracted with the red-headed Cinnamon. Just a few minutes later the police came bursting through the door with the informant coming out of the bathroom with his badge, saying that it was a bust. Robert, in a panic, said, "Genie, I wish for you to reverse everything that happened in the last 20 minutes."

The Genie granted the wish and they were just coming in the door to the room, and Robert saw the informant there. Robert pulled T.R.B. into the kitchen and said, "T, listen there is a guy in there who is going to ask you where you got the drugs from, don't tell him anything he's an undercover cop."

T.R.B.'s eyes lit up, "Who, point him out."

As Robert pointed the guy out, T.R.B. whispered something to his friend who grabbed the guy by the shoulder and asked him to come with him. Robert looked around thinking that everything was all clear, and began to wait for the strippers. The guy came back a few minutes after the strippers arrived saying, "Everybody, if that guy Simon tries to show up here, blow his damn head off, that sucka was wearing a wire."

Fearing that the police may still come, Robert got concerned. Robert decided there was only one way out of this, he said, "Genie, I wish to reverse everything for the last two hours." It was done immediately, Robert then pulled Genie aside where no one was around, "Genie, I wish for police to stop pursuing T.R.B. or anyone else that will be at the party that night." The Genie granted it, as the Genie wondered if Robert realized the danger in the wish he just made and if he had even the slightest clue that only 29 remained.

The next morning he woke up disoriented from all the drugs he had, he couldn't remember anything; he was on the floor feeling worse than he had in weeks. He called for the Genie, but the Genie was nowhere in sight. The Genie eventually came into the room with breakfast for everyone. When Robert asked him where he had been, the Genie said, "Fulfilling your wishes."

Robert suddenly realized the problem, he had made wishes when he was really high and didn't even know what he wished for. After saying goodbye to everyone and telling them all he couldn't wait for the next party he went to the hotel and wished for Genie to replay everything that had happened the night before when he had made the wish to stop the police.

The events appeared on the TV, and he saw himself dancing perfectly despite being high, then he saw the wishes being made one after another. He wished for a keg of beer, he wished for the stripper Cinnamon to have sex with him, he wished for T.R.B. to win a Grammy for rapper of the year, he wished for T.R.B.'s rival rapper, Big Money Playa, to screw off.

He began thinking about how to fix these problems; for starters, the other guys had seen the wish for the keg happen. So he wished for the Genie to remove anyone's memory of his wishes being granted. He also realized that the stripper Cinnamon might have had STDs or gotten pregnant. He wished for Cinnamon to not get pregnant by him and that any STDs get removed. He was trying to figure out another problem, he had wished for Big Money Playa to screw off. He asked the Genie what happened, the Genie informed him that since the term is used to mean to go away or in essence disappear that is what happened, Big Money Playa had disappeared last night.

In a panic Robert asked to see what happened and appearing on the TV was the footage of Big Money Playa doing a concert that night and literally disappearing mid song. Robert began to wonder how on earth he would fix this, he thought for a moment and then wished for Genie to undo that wish so that he never disappeared and no one would ever know he had ever gone except the two of them. As Robert calmed down he realized that he had had yet another unbelievable night and he had fixed all of this problems. All was well, he told the Genie that they were going home to rest and relax for a couple of days.

Robert took the airplane home and rested knowing that he was on top of the world and had the perfect tool that would allow him to stay there. The Genie waiting in his home looked out the window contemplating what the future held as he thought to himself, "Does he have any idea that he is down to

22 wishes, he has lost over two-thirds of his wishes and it hasn't even been two months?"

After they got home and Robert had all of his stuff placed where he wanted it he realized the one great problem that cleaning this house would be a nightmare. He couldn't trust a maid or maids because they might run off with his pile of money in the basement, or he thought they could steal pockets of money every day and he would lose many millions over the course of years.

So he had a brilliant idea, "Genie I wish for this house to clean itself every day, remove every bit of dirt, dust and grime in this house every single night at 2 am while I am asleep."

The Genie granted it, and Robert tried to figure out what he was going to do next. What else was there? He had won trophies, had partied with Playboy Bunnies, with rappers, and in painted cities red in Europe. He had to figure out what he was doing next, he suddenly realized he had not checked his e-mail in a few days and he was surprised that almost no one had contacted him. It struck him as odd that his old friends from his old job had not contacted him. However he began to think to himself, "I am going to have even cooler friends, I am going to be a star, the only question is how."

After a couple days at home he began to wonder how he would take full advantage of his incredible power, he decided that he needed to do something besides keep his money in the basement. However he couldn't let the general public find out about his wealth or let the government take half or more in taxes. So he began to look online about some ideas, he couldn't find any good options, he didn't know if he could trust any of the tax free zones. He began to get bored and decided he would go back to what always used to cheer him up: shopping. He took a whole bunch of money with him and he went on a shopping spree spending tens of thousands.

His spending did not go unnoticed by a couple of very attractive women, as they hit on him, he knew they were gold diggers but he didn't care. He looked past the greedy excitement in their eyes to their cleavage protruding out through their lower cut shirts. He wanted them both for himself and when he had a moment alone with Genie he requested, "Genie I wish for you to and stay within 20 feet of me at all times."

It was granted as he prepared for another very fun night with these women who were all over him. He took them out for a night on the town and quickly realized he should just stop worrying, he was set for life. They went to an expensive hotel and as they drank champagne in the deluxe hot tub. In the middle of another amazing night his cell phone rang. T.R.B. was calling to tell him that he had told a friend of his who was a film director about his dancing skill and he had a movie dancing coach role for him.

This added to his feeling of invincibility as he began to tell the women what he wanted them to do for his amusement. They were unsure when he suggested they begin having sex with each other, he rolled his eyes as Tamara said she wasn't really into that and he interrupted.

"Genie, I wish for Tamara and Suzanne here to do anything I say for the next 12 hours happily and to not remember me making this wish." It was done and the entire moment was replayed and they did what he commanded.

The next morning Robert was excited and asked if they wanted to come with him wherever he went so they could live the good life. They both seemed excited since they had been living with their wealthy parents, but said they would love to be kept women. Suzanne spoke up and said that while she would love to, but he would have to meet her parents. He knew right then that as exciting as having both of them would be, he would have to make several wishes to make sure that they wouldn't do anything that was inconvenient.

He wished that they would never hear or notice when he talks to Genie. He wished for them to never go into the basement where his piles of money were. He wished for their families to like him and encourage them to do whatever he said. He thought he was set now that he had a mansion, an enormous pile of money, two hot girlfriends and a Genie to do whatever he wished. He had the whole world by the tail, the only thing missing was his knowledge that he was down to 16 wishes.

The next couple of days went by as he wished for drivable replicas of all the Batmobiles ever created for film or television. He then realized some of them did not move very well, so he additionally wished for no one to even try to stop him from driving them. Driving down the street in a car that blasted fire only added to his ego and his feeling of invincibility.

While his life was very exciting and he decided that he wanted to go on another vacation, this time he was going all the way to Tokyo with Tamara and Suzanne. He thought that he would find out where all the hot-spots were and the three of them would have a hell of a time. Just as he was in the luxury suite celebrating, he got a phone call and walked into the bathroom to take it, so he checked to see who it was.

It was his Uncle Jerry, his first thought was, "I thought I wished for them never to worry about me or bother me for money."

The voice mail was not what he was expecting, "Hey Robert, look I don't know why you never visit your mother, and what you are so busy doing but she hasn't been feeling well lately and she finally went to the doctor and yesterday she was diagnosed with leukemia. So please come down to Sarasota and see her, she really needs to be with her family now."

He put down the phone and it began to sink in what had just been revealed to him. He peered out the bathroom door at the two beautiful women in his hot tub and asked himself, "How do I wipe this out so I can get back to my vacation?"

He called for the Genie, and he said, "Genie, I wish for you to remove any cancer that my mother has or ever had, so that my mother will be fine and the phone call that just happened didn't ever really happen."

The Genie accepted this and in no time Robert was back in the hot tub with Tamara and Suzanne eating chocolate covered strawberries. They all chuckled with delight while the Genie shook his head thinking to himself, "He has 13 wishes left."

Once again, they got drunk, very, very drunk and he woke up seeing the city being destroyed by a real life, over 200 foot tall Godzilla. He immediately panicked and told the Genie, "I wish for that thing to never have been created." As that wish was granted another monster was tearing up the city closer to where they were. "I wish for that bug thing, to never have been created." It was granted and everything was fine.

He left Tamara and Suzanne sleeping, completely passed out when he asked, "What the hell happened?"

The Genie responded, "You wished for a limbo stick, and when you lost, the girls told you to do something that would impress them, so you told them you could create Godzilla and you wished for it. You then told them you could make it more interesting and said you could have him fight a giant bug. Godzilla won just before you all passed out cheering."

Robert took a deep breath, "Does anyone remember Godzilla or that bug thing besides us?"

The Genie responded, "No, once you wished for them to have never been created you undid anyone's memory of it." Robert let out a sigh of relief that he had put out another fire and could go back to his vacation of a life.

He decided to wrap up his Japanese vacation early having gotten scared of the very close call. Tamara began to complain about why they were going home already when they had only been there three days and that he had better make it up to them with a trip to Acapulco. He didn't appreciate her nagging tone and began to wonder if she should be replaced. He decided that he wanted to do something different, somewhere else, alone, that way if he wanted to have sex with someone else they wouldn't complain. He didn't want to be tied down to two women.

He decided that he wanted some time away, so he decided he was going to take one of his Batmobiles and hit the road for Las Vegas. Shortly before he left, he found out where to put the gas in, he decided to make it the Batmobile from the Dark Knight Trilogy, even though it was too big for the road, he knew he would be fine.

Just before he left he wished that he would be left alone and no one would try to contact him and no one would come looking for him. The Genie who was in the passenger seat of the Batmobile shook his head, Robert was so caught up driving this enormous vehicle, the Genie knew Robert didn't see him. He wondered if Robert could see his remaining wishes dwindling away so that they were now at just 7.

As he got there everyone looked and stared at his Batmobile but no one dared tell him where he couldn't park, or what he couldn't do with it. It was as if he was single again after a mere couple of days, he was gambling, he was eating as much as he could at the buffets and he watched several stage shows. Those days were just amazing for him, he could drive like a maniac and no one would bother him.

There was one car that was moving slowly and he didn't appreciate being held up, he finally said to himself, "To hell with this guy," he then stepped on the gas made a sharp turn and ran the slow car off the road like it was nothing. An arrogant smile came across his face because he knew that no police would arrest him. No one would take his vehicle, he was set.

By the end of his third day, he decided to do something crazy and reckless, they were having a major boxing event tomorrow night and feeling invincible he asked himself, "What would happen if I beat the heavyweight champion of the world?"

He came up with what he thought were the perfect wishes to accomplish this: "Genie I wish for the challenger Miquel Davis to come down with the flu and be unable to compete."

The Genie granted this, he then followed with, "I wish for them to send someone to ask me to face the champion Terry Boulder and give me 25% more hitting power and double my normal thinking speed during each round." Sure enough within a couple hours someone representing the Nevada Boxing Commission told him that they needed him to face the champion tomorrow night.

The following morning he was brought in for a pre-fight interview where he proudly stated, "I'm Robert Selko, if you don't know who I am, you will after tonight. Terry Boulder your reign is up!"

He confidently threw a few fists towards the camera as the interviewer said, "No shortage of confidence here, will the dark horse conquer the champion?

We will find out tonight, back to you."

As the fight began, his increased reaction speeds helped him dodge several of the blows but his shots were not having the effect he thought they would, and when Terry Boulder landed an uppercut, he fell backwards, stunned. He got back up and tried to continue but he thought that he would barely be touched. After some more dodging and striking the first round ended, as he was trying to figure out how to win.

The second round happened and as he tried to go for a body shot he got clipped with a left, and was hit with a very hard right that knocked him down and made him disoriented. The referee counted him down for the count of ten as Terry Boulder held his world championship up making Robert boil with jealousy. This wasn't what he had wished for and he was going to change it, by any means necessary.

He came back to the locker room in an absolute rage, he called on the Genie, "Genie, I wish to undo everything that happened in the last 20 minutes and for me to have 4 times as much hitting power as I normally do in the rounds."

The Genie nodded and said, "It is granted."

This time when he went out there he already knew what his first few moves would be and hit Terry with a couple punches that left him stumbling. As he got back up Robert hit him a couple more times very badly and even after he fell he got on top of him and began throwing gloved fists while he was on the ground. The referee tried to pull him off but he was overcome with his jealous rage and the referee threw the whole fight out as he was escorted to the back.

Just as he entered the back area he wished for the last five minutes to be undone. The referee for the third time was giving his instructions and he knew that if he simply controlled his rage this would be a guaranteed win. The round began using his superior reaction time and extra hard hits he knocked out Terry Boulder in a minute and a half. The crowd stood stunned that this unknown person had just won the world heavyweight championship in such a one sided fight.

Despite his easy victory, he had one problem, the press he went to the post-fight press conference thinking he would be greeted as an underdog hero. The reaction he received was different than the glamorous one he had imagined beforehand.

The reporters began asking, "Who are you and how did you get this fight with no boxing experience?" Another asked, "How did you win a fight against a top tier fighter like Terry Boulder and barely break a sweat, did he get paid to take a dive?"

Robert did not appreciate these accusations and immediately walked out knowing no one would come after him. His thoughts raced with frustration, he felt like he had worked so hard at making these wishes work and all they could do was criticize. He began to think about taking all of the sports titles, gold medals in the Olympics, the Stanley Cup, the Superbowl, with the right wishes he could beat any team in any sport.

He spent the next two days relaxing by the pool in his hotel enjoying the Nevada sun, he began to look around for more sexual conquests and he saw a group of three women who were there with their company and he imagined another great foursome like he'd had at the Playboy Mansion. He quietly wished to the Genie, "I wish for the three of them to come up to my hotel room so we can have sex all night long."

As planned the three of them all came to his door that evening and began telling him that they had seen him by the pool and were very intrigued. As planned he had sex with all of them and they all left the following morning. He had enjoyed most of his vacation and was ready to take his Batmobile on the road and go back to his luxurious mansion in South Carolina. During his trip he passed into Northern Texas where he noticed things had gotten windy, but he kept on driving completely unaware of the tornadoes. As he continued driving, he came over a steep hill where he saw large twisters off the in the distance, he rolled his eyes at the inconvenience.

"Genie, I wish for no more tornadoes anywhere within 300 miles of me."

The Genie granted it and stared in disbelief that Robert was down to his final wish and he had given no thought to saving any of his wishes for an emergency.

The rest of the drive went as well as he could hope, he could run people off the road if they weren't moving fast enough, he was a God among men. As he got home, he called out to Tamara and Suzanne, they came downstairs and Tamara began acting nicer than usual.

"Baby, I have some great news, I got us a new friend, come out Cuddles, Cuddles come here." A Shih Tzu puppy came out of the kitchen and began barking at Robert, he bristled at this yappy little dog.

"Why did you get this yappy little hairball?"

Tamara said, "She's an adorable puppy that not only matches my wardrobe but look at that face, she needs love."

Robert just rolled his eyes; he had never liked animals and liked loud ones even less.

"Look Tamara, either you boot that thing out the door, or I am booting you out the door."

Tamara was disgusted, "You can't be serious!"

He responded, "Look peaches, I don't need you, you're only here for one reason, and I can find other women who are better than you anytime I want, so either ditch that thing or hit the road."

Tamara and Suzanne looked at each other with disgust as Tamara said, "Fine, we're both leaving." She and Suzanne went upstairs to pack their things, he apathetically sat there watching his jumbo sized TV waiting for them to leave.

The cabbie was helping them with their bags, Suzanne shouted, "You just threw away a great thing."

Tamara also yelled, "Enjoy being alone."

As the door slammed Robert was angry and wanted the last word as he told the Genie, "Genie, I wish to never see them again."

Feeling disappointed by this loss, as superficial as it was, he sat there for a few minutes until the show was over and then decided to go downstairs and look at his enormous pile of money, which was now neatly piles and piles of neatly stacked $100 bills. He looked around and he had an enormous smile on his face as he relished the possibilities, he decided it would be fun to make it rain and throw the bills in the air. However as he lifted some of the bills off one of the piles, his elbow accidentally tipped over several piles of the money on him as each pile fell like a small avalanche. It happened so quickly that it overwhelmed him and he could barely move. As he struggled, he barely poked his head out and his left hand. The Genie came down, once again becoming visible and returning to his original blue and green attire. The Genie looked at him shaking his head, as tears began to form around his eyes.

Robert cried out, "Genie I wish for you to get me out of this money pile... NOW!!"

The Genie looked at him and said, "You ran out of wishes. Never seeing Tamara and Suzanne ever again was your last one."

Robert became livid, "Are you kidding me, there is no way I am out of wishes!"

The Genie sighed, "Yes you are, you used up 70 wishes in three months. I cannot grant you anymore wishes even if I wanted to. Truth be told, I don't want to, you are childish, selfish and greedy, which is why I weep for us both."

Robert looked at him confused, "Stop lecturing me and get me out of here!"

The Genie lowered his head as he began to pace back and forth a few feet from Robert's head, "When we were in Ireland, you got mad at me for saying you were a fool. But I wasn't talking about you, I was talking about myself, I never wanted to be a Genie, if anyone knew what it entailed no one would. I was a sorcerer and I wanted more and more power. I hated remembering all of the exact incantations and speaking them every time, it felt time consuming and irritating. I was powerful, people came from towns away for my help, but I was greedy and wanted more and more until one day I thought I found a spell that would allow me to will whatever I wanted. I wanted it so badly I forgot that magic has to be spoken, if you aren't speaking you become the force being spoken to. That is why I am cursed with being a Genie, watching people like yourself repeat my mistake time and time again."

Robert said, "Get out, if you won't help me someone else will."

The Genie shook his head, "You wished for no one to come for you, no one to bother you, no one is coming until long after you are dead."

Robert responded, "I'll find my own way out, I'll show you."

The Genie said, "I doubt that, you can barely move and if you move too much even more of those piles will fall on you and smother you."

Robert in a rage said, "I'll show you, you Irish bastard!"

He tried to force movement only for the remaining piles of money to fall on him and bury him completely. The Genie began to walk up the stairs back towards his lamp, in a few minutes Robert Selko would die buried in his pile of money and when someone did come to look for him they would find his wealth his lifeless body and also the lamp that started it all. The Genie hoped his next master would break that cycle of greed and self-destruction, although he had been disappointed before.

THE EASIEST JOB IN THE WORLD

The new Prime Minister began a new initiative, it was a plan to guide the long term policies of the government. They were going to hire 10-15 philosophers to discuss the issues and how Canada should proceed with their actions.

Immediately, questions and criticism reigned from all directions, outraged people asking, "Why someone who read Socrates should decide tax policy?" Others asked, "How can the government waste $500,000 to $1 million a year for 10-15 people to just sit around doing nothing?" Some however saw it as the opportunity of a lifetime, "Do nothing but think about stuff, sounds like the easiest job in the world."

The applications poured in from all kinds of people as each was considered for their backgrounds both philosophical and not.

One of these people was Ralph Columbus, an Objectivist Libertarian, who had studied economics and whose favourite book was Ayn Rand's 'Atlas Shrugged.' Ralph was determined to set up a televised debate between himself and another member of the team. After some intense discussions, they agreed to it for four months after the launch.

Every day was painful as he received criticism from all sides, his colleagues, strangers, even members of his own family.

His cousin Rebecca was especially critical, "You're against universal health care but you take a full time living from the government, what the hell is that?"

Even his fellow libertarians wondered why he was taking a job being unproductive, referring to him as "part of the problem" and asking him questions like, "How is forcing me to pay your salary doing any good?"

What was even more painful were the online debates he was having and how many of his colleagues were relentless in ripping apart his arguments, and he had a very hard time dealing with the seemingly never-ending barrage.

Every two weeks he would go to the bank feeling almost dirty from the money he was getting but he kept trying to tell himself that when the time came for him to have his public debate, he was going to show the world how dangerous a big government was and he was determined that this would put the Objectivist Libertarian philosophy in the mainstream as opposed to the fringes where it had languished for so long.

One day he had a discussion with his friend Toby who had been reading Ayn Rand for the previous year and was hooked. "When you get to that debate, remember to mention that libertarianism and small government are not racist, in fact remember to mention that collectivism as a whole is dangerous, and that true libertarians think as Ayn Rand did that racism was the lowest form of collectivism there is."

Ralph seemed a little nervous, Toby asked him, "Are you scared for the debate?"

Ralph nodded and began to explain, "You see the Libertarian Party is still on the fringe, this is a golden opportunity to bring this to the mainstream and show everyone a better way."

Toby nodded his head, "Ralph don't be so nervous, you are a smart guy, you will leave them speechless or should I say blank out." They both let out a chuckle as Ralph was momentarily reassured that he was right and that this debate would be his to win.

As the date approached he replayed in his head the points he was going to make, as he did push-ups he remembered the words of his fictional hero John Galt: "It exists, it is real, it is possible, it is yours." Ralph always found those words so revolutionary, filling him with such motivation, filling him with focus and intensity in everything he did.

He always found the imagery of the cover of 'Atlas Shrugged' so powerful, the man who is carrying the weight of the entire world finally saying enough and casting it off. He had a sneaking suspicion of who his rival would be from the G.P.T., her name was Erica, she was an obvious democratic socialist who had repeatedly stated that a government has a duty to look after its people as much as it reasonably can and had made a video online about the benefits she believed would come from a $15 per hour wage and eventually instituting a living wage.

With just a month away the debate was on, Erica vs. Ralph, a socialist vs. a libertarian, the different schools of economics at war and at long last he was convinced that he was going to tear down every single one of her arguments. As he took deep breaths re-reading the entire book that had changed his life and he began practicing his talking points in 5 minute intervals to fit into the debate. He was initially told that they had only been able to get an hour subtracting the commercials and introductions he had lobbied for.

Just a few weeks before the debate he received a message from the organizers, in order to make it more viewer-friendly, the rounds were being shortened to 60 seconds with a 90 second final round so they could do several rounds each between commercials and the overall program was being shortened to 30 minutes subtracting commercials. This aggravated him, but at least he still had time to adjust. One of his few supporters e-mailed advice to him: "Watch out for the 'libertarians in the United States do this stuff' arguments make sure she doesn't draw you into that."

Ralph responded, "Don't worry, I can do this."

As the date drew nearer he was certain that he would finally show everyone that their faith in big government was misguided, that the free market was the best way and that his job for the last four months had not been in vain.

As the date neared he was stunned at the continued criticism, the most surprising accusations were from people accusing him of being a government pawn who is going to put weak arguments up against the socialist and who would give her all the excuses for Illuminati control. He was astonished, he was fighting the big government from the inside and the very people who were supposed to be rooting him on, were treating him like the other side in some sinister conspiracy. He decided he had to push past it and reach for the moment of greatness, his re-modeled arguments to fit into the 60 second frames were getting well-rehearsed and his delivery was becoming exactly what he was hoping for. He found out two days before that she would start, which was fine with him, he wanted the last word more than the first.

That day, he arrived at the building with less than an hour to spare, one of the TV producers walked him through the format he embraced it because he was ready to make history. It was as if John Galt had promised him this day it exists, it's real, it's possible all that was left was his victory making it his. He shook Erica's hand giving the basic obligatory greeting that all debaters have to as the cameraman gave the countdown with his hand '3, 2, 1' as the red light came on. The moderator named Pat introduced the topic, as Ralph looked at Erica through the corner of his eye looking for any fear or nervousness he had to stop himself from laughing at the irony of her being to his right.

As the debate began he waited for his turn as he had his pen and notepad ready to go. The moderator spoke, "Erica, why don't you get us started."

She began, "Thank you Pat, and thank you all for joining us here tonight, we know only too well how important these issues are people's personal and professional lives hang in the balance, I believe that a government of the people should do everything in its power to help the well-being of its people. We elect them every four years and they must be accountable to us, a government that does nothing in the face of disaster is a government that deserves no one's vote.

"I hope my opponent realizes this and I would be curious to hear what he has to say about this matter. I would also be curious to hear what he will say about the numerous examples of the free market failing to protect people's rights especially the vulnerable and minorities. I wonder what he will say about the regulations that have made our workplaces, food and water supply safer, our air cleaner and how the government of Canada has a competition bureau to prevent monopolies, these things are all things that are not done by a free market but by a government fighting for a free people, thank you."

He couldn't stop rolling his eyes expecting many of these arguments and almost being disappointed by the lack of challenge. "Ralph, your rebuttal," Pat mentioned.

"Thank you Pat, thank you all of joining us here tonight. There are numerous things wrong with what Erica said but I will start with the biggest one and work my way down. In a truly free market a monopoly is impossible because any company that tries to take advantage will have numerous people ready to take that market share from them.

"Let me make it simpler, If Coke bought Pepsi, other soft drink manufacturers would emerge to offer an alternative. The only monopolies are the ones governments set up and the idea that they emerge on their own in a free market is one of the biggest lies out there. Additionally, the government is not the solution to our problems but the cause of too many of them. A free market is the only true arbiter of value, the government should let the dollars in your wallet speak for themselves rather than taking them and wasting them foolishly and running up billions in debt.

"One more thing Erica, instead of lobbying for a $15 per hour minimum wage as you went on record to advocate and hindering the economy further, maybe not having so much income tax, sales tax and all the other ones would allow those who make $12 per hour to make their own dollars go further, thank you."

A smile came across Ralph's face feeling like he nailed it, exactly what he hoped for. As he looked at Erica's face he expected something more worried but instead she looked more confused than anything.

"Erica, your rebuttal," said Pat the moderator.

"Yes, yes, vote with your dollars, there is just one big problem the person whose parent's left them 50 million dollars regardless of their individual merit has more voting power than anyone close to being the average Canadian, unlike my opponent I believe in person one vote, not one dollar one vote.

"Secondly, while producing soft drinks is a cheap enough endeavour at least on the local level, I would argue that not all industries are so simple, there are capital expenditures called barriers to entry. I'm surprised that he forgot these things exist; after all he is the economist here. His side hates the government even when something isn't the government's fault, I mentioned earlier about racism, and the government in recent times have helped break the racial effect on people's ability to gain employment. There was a time when someone could be blatantly discriminated against on those grounds, now the person has recourse against these horrible practices.

"I also mentioned earlier about vulnerable people, but let's focus on children, how does the free market protect children? Quite frankly it doesn't, it only exploits them either as uninformed consumers or as labourers, either way it is dangerous and the stakes are too high to let our society go to the dogs."

Ralph shook his head, thinking, "Typical," as he cleared his throat for his round.

"Ralph, one more round for you before we take our first commercial break."

Ralph began sarcastically, "Oh how typical, the rich people have all the money and these poor people can't get any because the bourgeois are working the poor proletariat to death. All of this pleading, all of these decades of big government and what have you accomplished? Running up billions in debt plus interest on frivolous programs, try thinking of the children then. By the way, if you bring a child into the world it is your responsibility, a child's care is the responsibility of the parents above all else.

"As if I need to go on further racism is a collectivist philosophy not an individualist philosophy. Erica, I am sick and tired of this assumption that rich people didn't earn their money, they did, they worked their butts off despite the regulations, despite every other hurdle thrown in their way and they became successful. Instead of punishing success we should take away those hurdles that hold back other businesses and we would have a lot more wealth which would in turn make its way through the rest of the economy helping those that are looking for work or need more choice in workplaces."

Pat the moderator took the moment to remind everyone there would be more after the commercial break, the TV lights had begun to make him sweat as he took the cloth he had been given and began wiping the sweat that had formed on his brow.

He looked at Erica and saw her writing furiously, he let out a mild chuckle, "She's on the ropes and is starting to worry," he thought.

Before they came back from commercial, one of the producers said to him, "That was great stuff before the break. That passion keep it up, it's great for TV."

Pat the moderator said, "Welcome back everyone our debate is starting to heat up, we ended with Ralph so Erica it's your turn."

Erica nodded, "The bourgeois are not working the proletariat to death, but they used to until we gained greater worker's rights and I am amazed I have to explain this to you but I and most of Canada would agree that health care, education, infrastructure, police, the military, caring for the impoverished, the elderly, the disabled and the environment are not frivolous but essential to the well-being of people. As for the debt you have now brought up repeatedly, imagine if those wealthy people you are so fond of paid the tax that they should, those budget deficits would disappear.

"It would also be easier to collect tax revenue if major corporations had not spent the last four decades exporting jobs to places where people do not have the ability to demand the wages they can here. Last but certainly not least, while some people did become wealthy by legitimate means, why can't we create a system to make sure all have that opportunity. I would argue that expensive education does more to hinder opportunity and prevent new investment than all current government regulations put together."

Ralph began to bristle that she just couldn't let go of the notion that the corporations were the bad guys, he'd had enough of that. "Excuse me everyone, corporations don't force you to buy their products, but when it comes to government you don't have a choice, if you don't pay your taxes, you are looking at fines, or even jail time.

"That is blatant coercion for people to pay money into a system they don't understand, that they see minimal returns from if any. Also, this idea of 'if they only paid the tax they should' it will never be enough. If the wealthy paid 50%, people like her would say we need to finance this it should be 60%, if they got that they would then say we need to finance that, it should be 70%. The government will never stop, and re-distributing the wealth from producers to people who don't contribute is absolutely wrong, it may as well be theft and I think the hard working people of this country are tired of having their income stolen and given to unproductive bureaucrats and ineffective welfare programs."

Pat had an impressed look on his face, as if he did not expect this from Ralph, so he looked to Erica. "Erica, I think everyone would love to hear what your response to that is."

Erica let out a deep breath with a pause, "I would love to know what he thinks the government spends money on, because I can almost guarantee that he would get the amounts and proportions wrong. The money that gets collected in taxes doesn't go into someone's basement, it is distributed to those who need it and to programs that help people. Obviously asking government employees to work for free would be unrealistic, while there has been waste in public spending, this idea that the solution to this is to cut the budget like

64   CONFRONT THE RAVEN

they are obnoxious teenagers in a slasher movie, is not well thought out at all. How many companies would pave roads for everyone? I doubt any would, they would only do the ones that benefit their business directly the highways that you and I used to get here would not be there.

"One final point, people on welfare don't just sit around doing nothing all day, they use that money to sustain themselves until they get back on their feet. It is called a safety net, and if you want to know what happens without one, look something up, it was called The Great Depression. For years, people thought the free market would turn the market around but years went by and the downward spiral didn't stop. That's why we have a safety net and I'm glad it's there."

While there wasn't a live studio audience, Ralph looked at the various technical workers and saw them either unsure or nodding in agreement, he knew he had to beat this point right there.

"The Great Depression is where so much of this nonsense started, before then people didn't ask their government to make the economy better, they recognized that the government needed to stay out but we forgot that this last century. While people like Erica will tell you that everything got better after Roosevelt's new deal and the Canadian equivalents that were introduced soon after, the fact is, their measures barely did anything and the economy turned around because they spent an obscene amount of money on World War II. This was followed by an artificial boom, which occurred because many of our major competitors had been left in ruins. If we had the tax rates of back in the 50's today, our economy would be completely unable to compete and the idyllic world that socialists hold to would be nothing more than a childish fantasy." He felt like he won a few of them back with that point and awaited the squirming that he was sure would come from Erica. He turned to look at her as she rolled her eyes.

Pat the moderator took over, "That is a big statement, Erica your response."

Erica came across as bewildered at what she had just heard from Ralph, he took as a sign of her wearing down. "Oh yes, I have a response. While it was a temporary condition, a government should always use what it has to invest in its people, now more than ever we have to compete with knowledge, resources and infrastructure. During that time the governments of North America did some wrong things, but they also did a lot of building and investing in its people: we have never been more educated, illiteracy in its traditional form is almost extinct. The reason things aren't better is because after the period where the lack of competition ended, companies didn't invest in their people, they invested the cheapest labour they could. Rather than creating better products they made cheaper products and the automakers for example suffered the consequences later, but many of us have been suffering the consequences for decades. You mentioned an individualist philosophy versus a collectivist philosophy, while we are individuals we are also a society. Failure to recognize our dependence on each other, only leads to the old phrase, united we stand, divided we fall."

Pat turned to Ralph, "Last round before our next break, Ralph your rebuttal."

Ralph looked into the camera with an intensity that made him feel a foot taller, "Erica, did you really think you could duck the issue I raised and replace it with a cliché? Well guess again. For the last several decades the government has gotten bigger and bigger trying to come up with different ways to supposedly help the economy while increasing taxes and regulations hindering it. Whether it is the Keynesian idea of fiscal policy or the Milton Friedman idea of monetary policy, both have been exhausted and that is why Europe is so deep in debt that is why Canada and the United States are not far behind.

"We all need to go back to the 19th century way of capitalism, a capitalism that allowed you to try, succeed or fail, where budget surpluses weren't a memory and where people don't get their money stolen from them every pay cheque. By the way Erica, you argued against yourself when you talked about the automakers suffering the consequences for not making a better car.

"So here is a radical idea, stop interfering with the economy, it is not a car that you can make go a certain speed it is an ecosystem that needs to be left alone. Erica, let me offer one more radical idea, if you lose your job, go find another one and if you have trouble take steps to improve yourself so your market worth improves. Take responsibility for yourself, instead of asking big daddy government to foot the bill at the expense of everyone else."

Pat told the audience to stay right there as there would be several more rounds left, the camera lights turned off as Erica was writing furiously.

He tried not to snicker at her desperation, he tried not to make any indications that he was getting cocky.

One of the technical assistants asked him if he needed anything and he said, "A bottle of water would be nice." It was given to him a moment later, as he looked over his notes, wondering what direction Erica was going to go so he could cut her off at the pass. The director gave the countdown "5...4...3...2...1..." and the red light came on.

Pat the moderator started, "Thank you for joining us this evening this has been a spirited debate, but it is not over yet, we have six rounds to go and Erica, it's your turn."

"I am disgusted at my opponent, he wants to go back to the 19th century way of doing things? Apparently he either doesn't know or doesn't care that illiteracy was rampant, child labour not only occurred but could be very dangerous. The life expectancy of people was over 20 years less than today, while I'm sure they had no taxes, they also had far higher infant mortality and mortality in general, not to mention a blatant disregard for people's rights. Go look up categories of people called strike breakers and indentured servants.

"Even if he tried to amend the ways of the past to forbid slavery, how would a private education system not privilege the wealthy and leave the poor with little and the poorest with complete illiteracy and a complete inability to be anything more than the untouchables of our society? How would a health care system based on money not leave the poorest without the care they need, cough medicine is one thing, but open heart surgery can cost tens of thousands of dollars. How could an unregulated economy not lead to sneaky practices like the ones that hurt millions in the 2008 recession. You may want to go back to the 1800s, but most of us don't because we like the progress we have made, how the government helped facilitate it and I want to see what else we can do to make the world a better place for us all."

Ralph was surprised, he expected a far less coherent answer from his opponent, although he wasn't too fond of the personal attacks on himself. Ralph began, "This is where people get it wrong about Objectivist libertarians every time, we don't want the 1800s to return, we want a better world, the truth is the only way to get the best world possible is to allow freedom to be its driver, to let people choose a future for themselves. I have never heard any libertarian ever suggest a reintroduction of slavery or indentured servants, real libertarians care about the most vulnerable minority of all and that is the individual. When individuals pursue their own interests, they don't simply benefit themselves they benefit many of the people around them.

"Everyone in this room is benefitting at this very instant from the ingenuity of the people who invented television, microphones, and other various technical equipment that is allowing us to broadcast this across Canada tonight. Every single bit of it was done by people who had the courage to show what they could do and be remunerated well for it. Money is the driver of our economy and in many ways our lives, money doesn't make the world go around, but it sure makes it a lot more enjoyable. The 1800s that you look down on so much were a big improvement over the 1600s so imagine if we took that attitude to build on what we already have into the 21st century."

Ralph adjusted his tie, feeling like he had just crushed every argument she could possibly make, he could almost feel the applause from his fellow Objectivist Libertarians.

Erica looked through her notes to take page with a pink arrow attached to it as Pat said, "When you're ready Erica."

She began, "I would like to remind everyone, that every person in this room has benefitted from universal health care, and the people in this room benefitted from going to subsidized colleges and universities, I would also like to point out that just knowing that if you get sick, that it is not automatically a death sentence or a fast track to bankruptcy takes a great deal of stress off the minds of Canadians who have enough to deal with already. I would like to point something else out, while it is easy to think of me, myself and I all the time, and focus on individual problems, some problems are collective ones, the environment is the biggest one. If you ask who is responsible for climate change, you can't point to any one person, if you ask who is hurt by it, you can't point to one person, it is caused by and affects everyone and will continue to do so. So since it is everyone's fault, since it is a collective problem and hoping someone else will deal with it while I keep polluting is counter-productive.

"While my opponent might be able to name some examples of companies making more environmentally friendly products the truth is they have come decades later than they should have and the wide scale pollution that started all of this began in the era of unfettered capitalism that my opponent still idealizes. This problem reflects the problem of the Austrian school of economics that he appears to subscribe to, they focus so much on the individual, they don't add up what those individual actions meant in the macro picture."

Ralph was ready, he had expected the environment argument to come up, "Here is what my opponent completely misses, if there isn't enough market demand to warrant change, why would there be enough political demand? Jimmy Carter found out the hard way, in 1979 he called for things like mandatory conservation and asked over and over again for his fellow Americans to sacrifice and to use as little as possible. Then he was elected out of office the following year and replaced by Ronald Reagan who told Americans to pursue their self-interest. That was what the people wanted and the market meets it quicker than the government does.

"I would like add that private health care systems could benefit us in this room just as much if not better. Also if you want to take the stress out of people's lives, here is a great idea, stop the complete theft of people's money by the CRA, not only does it take away money that is rightfully someone else's but every time the CRA audits a person, they go back at least 7 years and make that person's life hell. Considering some of the audits are random that is a nightmare waiting to happen to many Canadians and could happen to some of the viewers this year. A socialist society has to keep collecting money and will resort to more and more invasive ways to do so to fund things that are supposedly for the greater good. Let the free market handle it, if you want it, eventually it will be built."

Pat turned to Erica, "This is the last round for our two debaters, this final round will be 90 seconds, so Erica your final statement?"

She brought the page with the pink arrow to the top of her pages, "What my opponent doesn't understand is that if political and market demand were the same, there would be no disconnect, but there is. The reason goes back to the fact that capitalists believe in one dollar one vote, and democratic socialists believe in one person one vote. An excerpt from a quote from Chris Hedges says 'unfettered or unregulated capitalism is about societies that cannibalize themselves, when capitalism is the dominant ideology, it turns everything into a commodity including human beings and of course natural resources. It exploits these commodities until they are exhausted and they are destroyed.' This is why a well-regulated capitalism with a proper social safety net is the best option, we can get most or all of the best aspects of capitalism without the worst effects that can't be understated.

"Repeatedly, I have asked my opponent about how his system would protect the environment or make sure that all have the health care and education they need. Repeatedly he has stated 'the free market will handle it' well I have one more question: what private firm would have researched it or even thought to identify the problem in the first place? The answer is they wouldn't but there is a lot of money in burying it for lucrative industries whose products are ingredient in the problem. The time has come for us to stop letting an irrational market filled with over exuberance, panics, short sighted bubbles and fraud convince us they are the ones responsible for prosperity. These shareholders will send a stock up if you let go of thousands of employees, the stock price also goes up if taxes are reduced, the stock price goes down if people start up new businesses creating more competition, and the stock price goes up when people are ready to spend. So where are the spenders supposed to get their money from if not from their employers, their own businesses or the government? This is like a farmer wanting to grow a bumper crop while using no water, the only difference is water occasionally comes down from the sky but money never does. In conclusion, regulations need to be maintained and improved upon because we need to put people before profits."

The buzzer sounded as Pat said, "Time's up, Ralph your turn."

Ralph had practiced over and over, this was the speech he had waited for, his last chance to leave a lasting impact on everyone watching at home. "Clearly my opponent has not been swayed by my arguments but I hope you at home have, we have some wonderful people in this country who work hard, innovate and create the things we love. When you adopt my opponent's world view you shut down those people, rather than letting them keep the wealth they earned and celebrating their work ethic and innovation, we take their money with one hand and slap them with the other.

"If we keep on this path the day may come when the producers ask themselves why bother and one by one they go on strike. That day has not happened yet, but it may one day soon, the way to prevent this is to stop expecting Atlas to hold the weight of the world on his shoulders and then wonder why his posture is harmed and why his back is hurting. The time has come for us to cast aside the misguided socialist ideas of the past that have led many countries to disaster among the most recent is Venezuela. The time has come to embrace the future of free market innovation that will reward hard work and merit and not how well you beg the government for help. I like many was inspired by Ayn Rand's classic novel Atlas Shrugged and would like to close with the John Galt words that have inspired me for years 'it exists, it is real, it is possible, it is yours.'"

With that Pat thanked the audience for joining them as the closing music ran and Ralph couldn't help but feel empowered, like he had begun something amazing, as if he had finally brought the Objectivist Libertarian movement to the mainstream. That night he went back to his hotel room and turned on his laptop, he was attacked from all sides, while some of them were strawmen arguments against him others were from his own side, claiming he slapped a philosophy that needed to be slain.

The following day he got a phone call from his friend Toby. "Hey Ralph, how are you doing?"

He responded, "I'm okay but disappointed, I am getting a lot of crap, even from our side. While I have gotten some encouraging comments, they are the minority. I don't get what is going on," Ralph said.

"Why, are you surprised?" Toby responded to Ralph's confusion. "We the taxpayers have been paying your salary not to mention the rest of the Government Philosophy Team for four months and all we got out of it was 8-9 minutes of you stating our position in a way that wasn't conclusive. Honestly, I'm your friend and I'm disappointed too."

Ralph began to get upset, "Are you kidding me, I had to jump through so many damn hoops just to get that half hour show on mainstream TV, I have been getting attacked from all sides and I was limited to one-minute rounds."

Toby said to him, "It's just not a good investment, it was a waste of money and you were part of it."

Ralph finally lost it, "Well sorry, I tried my best damn it, I'm only trying to…help….people." He paused overwhelmed that the cliché that he had heard a hundred times from his ideological enemies were now coming out of his mouth. He ended the conversation with Toby as he prepared for the long drive home.

His entire drive home, the five long hours all he could think about were those words he had said to Toby. He had spent years of his life despising the notions of sacrifice and altruism that Ayn Rand had attacked all those years ago and continuously until the day she died.

His thoughts raced: "There can be no contradictions, but I have been acting altruistically for the good of others even though that is the wrong thing to do, you are supposed to pursue your own interests. I was thinking so much about the political impact of a more libertarian system that I took all sorts of crap from other people and sacrificed my disdain of government bureaucracy and the possibility of a more lucrative job with an investment firm. Yet, despite this, I don't want to quit, I want to fight the current system, I am trying to help those taxpayers whose money keeps getting wasted and whose freedom to keep the wealth they rightfully earned. Yet I have taken a salary fighting for it from the very people I despise and had to fight on their terms. I know I am doing the right thing even though it is not in my best interest, even though this is altruistic, how can this be?"

He felt the philosophy collapsing on itself, a disconnection between two things that he was sure were right. He suddenly flashed back to the debate the moments when Erica was talking about an irrational market, he thought to himself, "Everyone wants to keep more of their tax dollars, tax lawyers are a big industry but the voting doesn't reflect it. Is my position any better than hers? Erica and I were doing the same thing, arguing for the greater good of the people and yet having opposite conclusions for how to accomplish this. Altruism was going through the both of us even though my philosophy forbade it, was Ayn Rand wrong at least about Altruism?

"Someone has to speak for the voters but no one wants to if they can make more money doing something else, leaving people who seem to have ulterior motives. The very people I was afraid of being mistaken for during the debate. Yet it has to be done and it should be done, which was exactly what Erica would argue about environmentalism or welfare or the regulations she believes in so much."

As he struggled with this for the hours that he drove, he began to think about a wholesale revision of his ideas and he began to fear what conclusion he would come to at the end. He knew he should go through with it but the implications would be enormous, it truly sank in that philosophy is a lot harder than anyone in the media was willing to talk about. Not only do you have to take on everyone else especially when your opinion is unpopular, but sooner or later you have to take on yourself. In that debate there is no moderator to say that's all, it just goes on no matter how painful or emotionally exhausting it is. As it turned out, the easiest job in the world wasn't easy at all.

A FATHER'S LOVE

It was another morning around the breakfast table, with two parents, two kids and one of the same old problems, the dad was talking about the family vacation.

"I think if we drive down we can see some historical sites and you can get a first-hand look at history."

His 9 year-old son Shawn spoke up, "Dad, you are so boring, you sound like my teachers."

He responded, "Every day is a learning experience, you should learn something new every day after all…"

Shawn and the 7 year-old daughter, Wendy, interrupted saying in sarcastic unison, "Knowledge is the lightest thing you can carry around."

The dad said, "Well I am glad you were paying attention, we have to get you to school. By the way we have to put a new hinge on the cupboard door today."

Shawn rolled his eyes he had a lot of other things he would rather do. As they got to school Wendy asked Shawn, "Shawn why is Dad so boring are other parents like this?"

Shawn responded, "No, Greg's dad just leaves them alone to watch TV and play video games." Shawn got to his class and noticed one of the kids wasn't there, but thought nothing of it.

That day Wendy and Shawn came home and waited for the inevitable boring lesson from Dad, he came home talking about accounting, decreasing liabilities, improving ratios, new revenue streams, what on earth was he talking about? Their dad started telling them about the tools they would need screwdrivers, screws and how he had measured the size of the hinge for compatibility. The kids were bored, their dad tried to let them put the screws in themselves but it didn't interest them.

"Remember lefty loosey, righty tighty."

Shawn blurted out, "Dad that is so lame!"

His father responded, "Lame or not, if it helps you remember something useful then use it." They finished installing the new hinge and Shawn couldn't get wait to the computer.

After Shawn logged onto Facebook one of his friends had posted that an Amber Alert had been put out for the kid who went missing, the comments section read on and on. Shawn was stunned that one of the kids that he had known for 2 years was missing.

One of the comments said, "Last I heard he said he had found something."

This was all the talk next day at school, "Where was Nick, who took him, is this a scam to skip school?" One of Shawn's friends Ripley had told him that she thought she knew what happened to Nick, a short guy in a vest that looked like armour told her that he could lead her to Nick. By this point Shawn had heard all the stranger warnings in the world from his Dad.

"Where did he want you to meet him?" She said that she would meet him in the forest at the creek.

Shawn said, "You have to tell someone, this could be a kidnapper, you could end up dead in a ditch."

She said back, "He could be the good guy and I might help him get Nick back, besides this is exciting."

Shawn looked at her in disbelief, "You shouldn't go alone, tell your parents."

She said, "He told me not to tell anyone, especially not any adults."

Shawn said, "Don't you know this is a trap?"

She said, "Fine, why don't you come with me?"

Shawn thought that they might need numbers, "Let me bring a couple friends, we will stay back and we'll catch this guy." Over the course of the day he told his two closest friends Patrick and Lyle and they decided that the four of them together could ambush the short man in a vest.

The short man in armour had suggested 4:30pm, so Ripley was there with the other kids a few dozen metres behind her. As she approached the creek she nervously looked around, hoping that Shawn was wrong and that this wasn't a trap. She waited for a few minutes.

Lyle whispered to Shawn, "When do we jump in?"

Shawn said, "The second she calls for help, we book it."

Patrick kept looking around, "Where is he, I can't see where he's coming from?"

Suddenly a bright green light emerged and two small men in armour emerged from the tunnel that was there and then a button was pressed and the tunnel closed. As one of them looked around, the other one said, "Come with us, and you will see Nick."

She became scared, "Where is he?"

The one who was speaking took tiny steps closer, "He's fine come with us and we will get him back to this world."

She became more upset, "Where is he?"

The one who was speaking said, "Our world." He was now within arms-reach and grabbed her, she immediately screamed when the other one pressed a button turning the tunnel back on.

Shawn blurted out, "Let's get 'em." As they ran, the two short men in vests leaped into the tunnel with Ripley and it closed just as Patrick leaped over the creek and he ran into a tree.

"Crap," Shawn said with frustration, "we have to tell our parents, this is serious, they got her."

As Shawn came home his mother asked him where he was, he was an hour and a half late from school. He said he had to talk to both his mother and his father, she looked at him, "Oh no, what did you do?"

Just then his father got home with some grocery bags with his usual, "How is everything going?"

The mother said, "You arrived just in time for a major confession."

His father said as he sat down at the kitchen table, "Okay Shawn, what's going on?"

He took a deep breath, "Mom, Dad, Nick went missing and a short man told Ripley that he could take her to him and me Lyle and Patrick went with her to the forest to protect her and then this other guy came out of some portal and took her before we could save her."

The mother put her face in her hand as the father immediately stood up began to get upset.

"Hold on a second, one of your classmates was invited by a stranger into the middle of nowhere and you took two of your friends with you and now she's missing? Oh my god! You could have been kidnapped, what were you thinking? Why didn't you tell us, or your teachers? Or the police?"

Shawn spoke up, "We thought we could catch him."

His father became even more upset, "This isn't a game, we have talked about this! Repeatedly!"

Shawn tried to speak up, "Dad they had some portal."

His father was having none of it, "I don't care what superpowers you say they have, this is dead serious. Go to your room, right now."

As he was walking back to his room, he heard his father saying to his mother, "I am not being too harsh, until we find out what is happening he is not going off on his own."

Shawn had rarely seen his Dad so upset he was normally so happy and boring.

As he went into his room he went onto Facebook and Patrick asked him what was happening. He told him about the conversation with his parents, then Patrick said that he was left a note on his window that said that all 3 of them had better show up to the back area of the park or they would never see Nick or Ripley again. He knew he was grounded, but he believed he had no choice, so he Patrick and Lyle messaged back and forth to figure out what they would do.

The next morning, Shawn was pulled aside by his father and he said to him, "listen Shawn, I am coming home early so I can be here when the police arrive here this evening, Ripley never came home last night and they want your statement. Listen son, I know I yelled last night, but if something ever happened to you, Wendy or your mother I would never forgive myself. I need you to be completely honest, no superpowers talk, this is a very serious situation and there are some bad men out there doing bad things. We need to help the police to find your friends, this is a situation that I know is hard to deal with, but we need to do this, okay?"

Shawn gave the obligatory okay and left for the school bus.

During lunch, Patrick, Lyle and him met to talk about how they would handle what was sure to be an ambush awaiting them in the park at 5:30pm, they decided to pack some weapons hoping they could fight back against the short men, who were still bigger than them.

Lyle spoke about something his older cousin had told him. "He told me that if you ever have to fight for your life, put something in your hand like a roll of quarters to fill your fist and when you punch, you will knock the suckers out."

Patrick said, "I hope we don't need a knife to hold them up with."

Shawn said, "I'll bring those."

They went home preparing for a daring rescue mission, with Shawn knowing that he would have to sneak out to do it.

Shawn came home before 4:00pm as usual and began to look for everything he would need, he had told Wendy to watch TV so that she would not know that he was up to something. As he prepared like so many of the superheroes he had seen in the movies he had seen, he was picking up the butcher knife when Wendy had walked in to get something to eat.

"Shawn what are you doing?"

He tried to cover his tracks, "Nothing, go away."

Wendy knew better, "You are up to something, if you don't say so I will tell mom and dad."

He reluctantly agreed, "Okay but you had better not tell them, do you swear?"

Wendy said, "Cross my heart."

Shawn then said, "Okay, I'm leaving for the park, I have to get there by 5:30pm. Patrick, Lyle and me know who the kidnappers are and we are going to get them back."

Wendy's mouth was opened a mile wide, "Mom and Dad are going to kill you, you're not supposed to go anywhere besides school, you're grounded!"

Shawn responded back, "You swore don't tell them!"

They heard the door open, "Okay, now that's mom don't say anything, I have to leave soon."

After their mother got home, she gave them both a hug, "Hey kids, where is Judy?"

Wendy said, "I don't know, we came home and no one was here."

Their mother rolled her eyes, "That's the second time, this has happened. Why is a good babysitter so hard to find?"

Shawn waited patiently in his room for the right moment, each minute made him a little more nervous, by 5:00pm his palms were sweaty. Just after their father came home, he knocked on Shawn's door and came in, Shawn turned the other way for fear that his father would see the look on his face and know he is up to something. His father saw him curled up on his bed facing the wall.

"Look Shawn, I know you are upset with me but this is really important, the detective will get here at 6 and we need you to tell him everything you saw. I'm going to go get changed and then we will have some dinner."

Shawn knew that he wouldn't get away then, as soon as his Father's door closed he packed the last things he thought he would need and he ran as fast as he could out the door, just a moment later his father came out of his room in his more casual clothes and opened his son's door to see nothing.

He began to call out to him, "Shawn, Shawn? I can't give dinner to someone who's hiding." As he came downstairs he asked his wife if she had seen him.

She said, "No, I haven't seen him since he went to his room."

He noticed Wendy trying to hide, "Wendy, do you know where Shawn is?"

She said in a very nervous voice, "I don't know, I'm sure he is doing something good."

Their father took a deep breath, "Honey, you know how Shawn sometimes tries to do something he isn't ready for?"

Wendy responded, "Yeah, like when he tried to start that campfire and burned his finger?"

He responded, "Exactly, he might be doing something like that, but even more dangerous, please where did he go?"

Wendy said, "I promised I wouldn't tell."

Their father said, "Honey, you made a promise that you shouldn't have, please tell me."

Wendy finally said, "Shawn, Patrick and Lyle are going to the park to take on those kidnappers. He even took your big knife."

The mother blurted out, "Oh my god," their father immediately gave her a big hug, and began to rationalize the situation.

"He only left a couple minutes ago, he's on foot, I am getting into my car and I will get him back."

The mother then pushed him away, "Then go get him! Now!"

Their father rushed to the car with his heart racing, his adrenaline pumping and the fear of losing his son racing through his mind.

As his father's car was on its way Shawn arrived with Patrick and they waited for Lyle, they whispered to each other, "Do you have everything?"

"Yeah, do you?"

The other responded, "Yeah."

As they looked around Lyle got there, "Okay, where are they?"

Patrick said back, "Nothing yet."

As they looked around they began to go back-to-back-to-back ready for a battle. Just as Shawn's father pulled his car up to the parking lot, the green portal opened up and out came the short men in armour, six of them as well as man dressed in a long purple robe with demon's faces stitched onto it. His large moustache and his staff with the glass ball on top indicated his authority and how fearsome he was.

"Get them now," the guards charged but the kids began to fight.

Shawn was picked up and he kicked one of the guards in the face, which sent him backwards hitting his head off the metal pole of the fence knocking him unconscious.

Their weapons were quickly overpowered as one of the guards asked, "What about him, Emperor?"

Before he could respond the glass ball on top of the emperor's staff began to flash red. "Leave him, we must leave, someone is coming."

They opened up the portal with a remote and Shawn's father came over the hill just as he saw his kids being carried away, he ran so fast but fell short. He slammed his fist onto the grass in rage.

"God damn it!"

He went closer trying to make sense of what happened when he saw the one that was unconscious starting to come to, his eyes flared up as he was ready to get answers by any means necessary.

Despite the continued struggling of the kids, these five men who were four and a half feet tall were too much for them as the emperor opened the door of his temple.

As he motioned for them to come in Shawn yelled, "We're going to get you, you ugly asshole."

He began to laugh, "That won't happen, you see children like you are brought here for one reason, your young blood."

As he pressed another button pushed forward and shifted to the left showing several children unconscious, in large bags with blood slowly coming out of the bag in a tube. Patrick suddenly began struggling and began to wrestle himself free when one of the guards holding Lyle let go of him and punched Shawn in the face knocking him down.

Shawn blurted out, "You're never going to get away with this, the police will come after you."

The Emperor looked at him with a glare. "You don't get it you stupid child, we are in a pocket dimension the police couldn't get here even if they knew it existed, no one is coming to save you, I am going to use you and the rest of the children to guarantee my immortality. Hook them up to the drains until they are unconscious before we package them."

Completely overwhelmed and having no idea of what to do he began to wish for someone to save them, anyone, anything he just wanted to wake up from this nightmare. As they began to get locked onto the wall and they were starting to rip the sleeves off their shirts Lyle began to cry and beg.

The emperor turned his head, "How pathetic, I will be glad when he is packaged."

Just then the front door opened and Shawn's father stood there holding the guard that had been left behind by the throat.

The guard had bruises on his face and was yelling and pointing, "They are right there, right there."

Shawn's father let him go and said, "Run," and the guard ran for his life.

The Emperor stood in disbelief as Shawn's father said, "So you're the son of a bitch that kidnapped those kids! I'm taking them back." Shawn's father had the eyes of rage as he walked into the temple fists balled up looking like a man on the edge of savagery.

"Guards get him!"

Shawn yelled, "Dad look out!"

Shawn, Patrick and Lyle all looked at the door with shock. The first guard charged and Shawn's father threw a single hard punch that knocked him down as two others grabbed for his arms and he elbowed one in the face and threw his forearm at the other. He then threw the one he had elbowed at the other two, he punted one of the guards in the head and stomped the other repeatedly. The first one he had punched tried to strangle him from behind as he flipped him forward and kicked as hard as he could into that guards back.

The Emperor was stunned and afraid, one of his guards was getting back up and Shawn's father grabbed him and dragged him towards the door and threw him down the stairs. Two of the guards got back up and tried to knock him down the stairs but he only fell a few steps when they kicked him in the head and began to beat him at the top of the stairs.

"Bring him back in here," the Emperor commanded, as his two guards began to pull him in. He turned to the three captured children, "You, this is your father this is what happens to those who defy the Emperor."

Shawn's father had a sudden burst of energy as he began throwing fists and arms and knees as quick as he could as the Emperor struck him in the back with his staff and he fell against the wall.

Patrick turned his head to Shawn, "Your Dad is going to die if we don't do something."

Shawn looked around for something to help them but his eyes were drawn to his father struggling to fight off everyone. He threw a fist at one guard and then took down the Emperor but as he had just begun fighting when the other guard would restrain his arm and try to choke him. Shawn looked at his cuff and saw that it was bolted to the chain. He realized his cuff had not been completely secured as he tried to wrestle his left wrist free, his desperation grew as he saw his father struggling against the numbers.

He finally got his left hand free when he heard the Emperor say, "I'll kill you."

Shawn heard his father yell back, "You're gonna have to!"

Shawn began to turn the bolt on the cuffs on his right hand remembering his father telling him, "lefty loosey, right tighty." As the cuff came off he went to get Patrick's free, just as it was coming loose he saw the Emperor hit his father in the right knee with his staff causing him to fall over. By this point everyone was bruised and bloody. He kept turning and told, "lefty loosey, right tighty," to Patrick so he could free his other hand. He was turning the bolt loose on Lyle's cuff as he saw his father throw a hard kick seemingly knocking out one of the guards, but the one that had been thrown down the stairs had come back.

Just as all of them got free, Shawn's father was on being forced to the ground and the other two guards and the Emperor picked up his staff to begin the assault. Shawn, Patrick and Lyle charged and attacked the two guards forcing them to release Shawn's father. Shawn was kicked down by the Emperor, when a bloody and enraged father charged and once again took down the Emperor as one of the guards came to get him. Shawn's father picked up the staff and swung it like a baseball knocking the guard unconscious as the Emperor got on top of him to choke him.

The Emperor proclaimed, "You will not stop my immortality!" when he was forced off and Shawn's father began a relentless assault.

"I will stop you, you kidnapping monster."

Patrick had picked up the roll of quarters he had brought with him and after a few punches and the guard seeing the kids outnumbering him and seeing Shawn's father beating the Emperor he ran.

Shawn turned after seeing the guard leave to see his father in pure rage beating the Emperor to death, the Emperor was now defenseless when Shawn called out to his father and his father looked at his son, immediately his rage began to subside and he stopped looking at the Emperor's unconscious face. Shawn's father got back up, bruised, scratched and bloody, he took a couple steps then he fell to his knees and opened his arms to his son who ran into them. They hugged as the father's savage demeanour had melted into relief of having his son back.

Lyle mentioned the kids who had been captured and they went through the Emperor's robe and found the robe that opened the door. They slowly took the children out, carefully removing the tubes that were extracting the blood. The children that were there were almost lifeless and they opened portal to the park. Where they took the Emperor back with them so that he would face justice.

The next day the newspapers were buzzing, the news reporters had a million questions, but those weren't the questions that Shawn's father was worried about, he was far more worried about the questions his son would have. They had been to the hospital, the police station and they hadn't slept all night.

The following day Shawn didn't go to school and his father didn't go to work. Around 3 pm Shawn's father woke up and went down stairs to his basement with the pool table and began knocking the balls while he tried to figure out how to answer the numerous questions his son would have.

Around 5 pm Shawn woke up and came downstairs, "Dad, where are you?"

His father yelled out, "Down here son, playing some pool."

Shawn came downstairs, "I can't believe I was up so late."

His father responded, "Yes, I couldn't believe how late it was either."

He gave Shawn a pool cue as he began to take the balls out of the pockets. "Son, there is a lot for us to talk about and it's been a really rough last couple days. So if there is anything you want to talk about please tell me."

Shawn hesitated but then looked at his father and asked, "Why did he want our blood? How would that make him immortal?"

His father responded, "People used to believe a lot of crazy and dangerous things that was one of them. Putting powerful technology in the hands of primitive minds can lead to terrible things." There was a pause before his father continued, "Is there anything else you wanted to ask?"

Shawn reluctantly responded, "Dad, all these years you were boring and suddenly it was like you turned into someone else. I mean you kicked ass, but it was so weird to see you like that, it was... scary."

Shawn's Father took a deep breath, "Shawn, the world isn't always a nice place, in fact there are some really bad people in it."

"Like the Emperor?" Shawn asked

"Exactly, there are several types of bad people that your mother and I want to protect you and your sister from. When you have children, you always hope that they will have it better than you did and the thought of someone hurting them not only scares you it can bring out something that you almost forgot that you were ever capable of. I just hope you know that I would never do anything like that to you, your sister or your mother."

Shawn responded saying, "I know you were trying to protect me, and you saved me, Patrick, Lyle and the others."

His father responded, "Patrick, Lyle and I, grammar is important." Shawn rolled his eyes his father continued, "See I'm still the same old Dad."

They hugged and played a couple games of pool, as that day Shawn learned lessons that he would remember for the rest of his life. First, what can happen when power falls into the wrong hands, second that a great parent will go beyond the edge of the earth for their kids and third that love and hate aren't as far apart as we think they are.

THE HUNT FOR HITLER

On February 22, 1945 8 men were selected from their divisions for their skills and/or knowledge of the German language to meet for a top priority assignment. It began with General Hondo coming in, and setting up a basic projector screen with slides. As all 8 of them came in, General Hondo asked them all to take a seat. As he got all of the slides in the correct order he stood next to the projector screen and asked all of them if they were ready, they all nodded.

"Very good, if any of you have to piss, you better do it right now because I don't want any interruptions."

No one got up as a few tense seconds went by. "Great, we will proceed. As you all know, the last several months have been successful for our side, we have taken back a great deal of land from the Nazis and we are closing in on the capital, Berlin." He changed slides to show a map of Germany and the surrounding area coloured to indicate the current occupied areas.

"This war has been going on a long damn time and the odds of us being victorious this year look very likely, unfortunately we have one enormous problem. We aren't the only ones closing in on Berlin, we are closing in on it from the west and the Russians are closing in on it from the east in fact if current trends continue, there is a strong chance they will get to it before we do. Unlike our other friends the Canadians, or the British, who we are confident would take this son of a bitch out, we can't trust the Russians that much, they were Hitler's allies during the beginning of this war and they don't give a damn about the freedoms we have. The only reason we work together is our common enemy; that will change with the end of the war."

He changed the slides again to show pictures of Stalin speaking to his people. "The last thing we need is Hitler either being protected by Stalin or worse yet, being allowed to advise them on their future policies and leading them to come after us. Make no mistake the Russians are a potential threat, if Hitler gets in Stalin's ear, we might end up having to fight them for years to come." The slides were changed again to show a picture of a German line. "So we have to get to him first, that is why you are here. We want you to sneak behind enemy lines and you have one simple mission… capture or kill Hitler. If you can capture him, hold onto him with everything you got. If you can't and you have to kill him, shoot him as many times as you have to so that there is no way in hell he ever gets back up. If anyone doesn't think they can do this mission, the door is to your left, if you are ready to risk your life to break their machine then stand up and take these booklets that have been prepared for you.

"Every one of you was chosen for specific reasons, many of you have stellar records, six of the eight of you are fluent and German and have additional skills, the other two have at least a passing knowledge and you had better study hard. So remember if you leave we have to find someone less qualified to replace you."

All of the soldiers looked at each other as they got up and headed towards the booklets, with each passing step Scott knew that in those booklets were the directions that would lead him and the others to glory.

He took the booklet back to his barrack knowing the mission was a long shot, and as Scott read through the plans he saw why. Hitler was protected very well and while they had a few codes to work with it was still a serious risk. Thankfully six of the eight of them were fluent in German which would give them an advantage and each would be provided with authentic German combat gear. A handful of spies had been helping to collect information on taking out Hitler and had met with gradual success. Scott put down the booklet every few minutes to imagine the glory of him and the others winning a medal of honor on a large stage with thousands of people applauding them. The imagined glory to come filled him with excitement, Scott Connor, the man who took down Hitler, a war hero and a role model to Americans from coast to coast. His daydreaming never lasted too long as he had to prepare for the real day which was March 15th that year.

As they prepared for the mission General Hondo met them at the base. "Men, as predicted we are getting closer and closer to Berlin, but so are the Russians, I can't stress enough how important this mission is, have you all read that booklet?"

All eight of them nodded.

"Did you memorize that mission through and through so that you could recall it in your sleep?"

They all nodded.

"For the two of you who are not fluent in German did you practice the common phrases you are expected to know and the standard responses you will need?"

Scott and another soldier named Michael nodded.

"Very good. I am sorry to say that even if this mission is a complete success it is virtually impossible that all of you will be coming back. So whoever does make it back, I will buy you a drink, and those who don't, you will not be forgotten. Now strap up your boots and go get that German S.O.B."

As they got into the chopper to the entry point that they could smuggle into, Scott had a smile from ear to ear. This was the beginning of the moment he imagined in his head, celebration, victory, glory and most of all the respect and admiration of his peers. Across from him was Dale, who looked concerned.

"Hey Dale, is it?" Scott asked.

"Yeah I'm Dale," Dale responded.

"What are you so nervous about? We are lucky, we have been chosen to be the eight guys who win the war."

Dale looked at him, "I know the mission, I know plan A, plan B, plan C, and I hope I don't have to kill myself as part of plan D."

Scott looked puzzled, "Don't even think about Plan D, we are the best of the best, you're the medic here even if we get hurt you have us covered right?"

Dale nodded but wasn't reassured. "I'm worried because I am fluent in German but I am worried that they might hear an accent, the same way that if they tried to speak English we would hear their accent. I would hate for that to tip them off and ruin the mission. I know that thousands of soldier's lives are riding on this."

Thomas spoke up, "Don't be so nervous, they're like animals, if they smell your fear, we are screwed. Besides, we have five other people speaking fluent German on this team. Keep your eye on the prize. And by the way Scott, I hope you are as good of a shot as the booklet claims because if we get ambushed the clock will be the enemy."

Scott looked at him, "Trust me I am a good marksman, and if we can't get him alive, I won't hesitate to kill Adolf dead."

Rusty chimed in, "I sure hope so because I don't want to have to walk up to General Hondo and say the Russians got him. I don't know about the rest of you, but for me I got two options, victory or death."

The de facto leader of this group was Thomas who tried to imitate General Hondo's demeanour, with mild success, "As you all know, we will be sneaking into Lower Saxony, we have to get to the Bergen Belsen camp, so we can then be transported on Saturday into the interior, once we get transported they will most likely be taking us to Strausberg on the eastern side to fend off the Russian advance, once we get there we have to meet with our contact who will hopefully smuggle us back to Berlin where we will be going big or going home.

"Remember, no matter how much you want to vomit, no matter how much you hate it, don't interfere with Bergen Belsen's operations, the people in there will be freed soon and they will stay free if we finish the mission."

They all nodded as Scott thought to himself, "It will be hard but it will be worth it," as he once again briefly envisioned the award ceremony that he was sure would await him.

As they came in, their false suits and credentials managed to fool the camp's organizers who were short staffed since the last few months had thrown their operations into disorganization. Each day as Scott saw the abject misery in the eyes of those people it nearly drove him mad that he couldn't help them. It took every bit of restraint he had not to shoot the real guards and throw open the doors.

On the morning of Friday March 23rd, Dale and Scott were ordered to dispose of the carcasses of three people who had tried to escape and had been shot off the walls. While Dale had seen death on the battlefield before this was very different, they picked up the bodies to put them in the ovens.

Dale whispered to Scott, "This is just wrong, I mean I've had to take away dead bodies before but they at least got a burial, they were wearing uniforms, they had weapons with them. They signed up and could fight back. This... this is just, this must be what hell is like."

As tears began to form in his eyes as one of the guards came by, "What are you crying about?"

Scott answered in his imperfect German, "The smell."

The German guard walked up to Dale saying in German, "Toughen up, we are doing what must be done."

After he walked on Dale looked at Scott and said in a hushed tone, "Thanks, I know you were trying to save me, but you need to be more careful you almost blew our cover."

Scott looked around and whispered, "You are the one who is crying. Look this is awful, but we are getting out of here tomorrow so just grin and bear it."

Dale looked back at him with confusion, "How can this not make you sick?"

Scott began to pick up the second body, "I block out and do what has to be done. I hate wearing this uniform, I could barely look at myself in the mirror this morning but I bite the bullet so we can finish the mission."

Dale shook his head, "That's what he just said a minute ago."

Scott rolled his eyes as he got the body onto the slab, "Maybe but when

I'm done with my job those poor souls who are still alive will go home and the world will see us as the heroes who broke this killing machine." Just before pushing the body in Scott looked down and saw the man's eyes and mouth open, his eyes were staring at him as if to accuse him. Scott had stop himself from being caught in the trance of those haunting eyes.

The next day the truck came by to pick up the soldiers who had been transferred there temporarily including the eight of them. As they were driving one of them who was fluent in German began telling a joke and was using a hand signal to tell those who weren't when to laugh. The few days in Bergen Belsen had taken a great toll on all of them but Dale above all could barely hold back the horror of what he had witnessed.

Scott pulled Thomas aside, "I'm a little worried that Dale is going to do something stupid, I thought he was going to do something stupid and expose us. Look that place is horrible but he almost couldn't handle it."

Thomas whispered to him, "He mentioned it to me, I told him that if he needed any more motivation to do this mission he just needed to remember that if the Germans win, some place like that could be set up outside Minneapolis. I think that fixed him right up."

Scott nodded his head, "Sure works for me."

As planned they were shipped to Strausberg, where the Russians were advancing, the plan was to bide their time for their contact who had the names of the eight of them and would say "Adler" which was German for Eagle. If they responded back with their code word he would know he was talking to the right people. As the fighting began the eight of them were keeping their eyes open waiting for someone to tell them "Adler" the afternoon went on, as the shots continued to be fired.

Thomas knew something was wrong and knew that they were losing ground he saw the Russians coming and knew that if they stayed they would either be captured or killed and all would be lost. Scott threw a grenade to stop two of Russians that were coming over No Man's Land, just as he turned to Steve to ask for more bullets he saw that he had been shot dead. He looked and saw Thomas crawling on the ground who waved for him to come with him, one of the other Germans looked at him leaving and Scott said, "More bullets," in German and let out a cough to make it look like a cold was the explanation of his voice sounding off.

Thomas had gathered the others and told them that they were leaving.

"Where's our contact?" Rusty asked.

"He didn't make it and apparently Steve and Walter didn't make it either. It's the six of us going to Berlin on our own. The plan is now out of the goddamn window." They ran for it, thankfully covered by a supply tent that the German contingent had set up.

"So where do we go?" Scott asked.

Thomas took out his compass, "We are going south and then west, we got 24-25 miles to go and somehow someway we have to get there." As a large explosion hit the front of the tent, he said, "Now, now, due south, get past the lake and go west, now, now, now."

They fled as fast they could as if they were running from the Grim Reaper himself. Dale pulled his compass out of his pocket, to verify they were going south, they were going slightly west, but at this time it was a moot point as bullets were being fired behind them. They continued to run as they felt themselves getting shorter and shorter of breath, they finally pushed themselves to keep running to an area under a big bridge. They all stopped as they were hunched over catching their breath, they all looked at each other, completely overwhelmed by their situation.

Michael spoke up after they all began to get their composure, "What now?"

Thomas looked around at the men who had doubt in their eyes, "Michael, Rusty, Dale, Scott, Jack, I know you have spent weeks studying your booklets, you have prepared for the plans, well, now our plan is out the window. We have one decision, do we figure out a new plan or do we give up?"

Rusty said, "Okay, let's come up with a new plan, any ideas?"

Scott added, "Well we are several miles from Berlin, if we walk we can get there in a day or so."

Dale's eyes nearly burst from his head, "We might not have that long."

"What do you mean?" Rusty asked.

Dale responded, "If our contact didn't show up, it might be because he was found out, he might squeal to save his life and if so they might be looking for us."

There was a moment of stunned silence.

Thomas finally spoke, "Okay we don't have the facts and we don't have a way to contact the outside as long as we are in Germany, we have to be extremely careful, as they might know some if not the entire mission."

Scott interjected, "Even if that is the case, we have one thing going for us, he didn't have the booklet. He only knew he was meeting American soldiers with the code word so they won't know our names or what we look like, right?"

Thomas paused, "No he did have names, but he didn't have our pictures, that is our one shot. So from here on in, if you hear someone who is looking for Americans or uses 'Adler,' don't engage, it may be trap, agreed?" One after another they all agreed and Thomas looked at the compass, "Okay due west, Berlin or bust." They all nodded their heads, everything from this moment onward was uncharted territory.

They began their long march, the march to Berlin. As they continued to the west Scott spoke to Dale.

"Do you think this is going to work?"

Dale responded, "I am hoping that there will be so much chaos that we will be able to slip through. I am hoping that if we remain inconspicuous and don't try to look for means of communicating to the outside we can slip through."

Scott said to him, "We are going to have a hell of time getting out of this country, I will be so glad if we capture Hitler and get him across the border. I will never be happier to see the French."

Rusty let out a chuckle, "Same here."

As the sky became darker the clouds were getting greyer and thicker, Thomas looked up saying to the men, "Men, we are going to have to find some shelter the last thing we need is hypothermia driving us into the Nazi infrastructure." They came across an abandoned house in the country that had the windows broken into, with no one nearby they decided this would be the perfect place to stay the night, provided they block the windows to keep the possible rain out. That was going to be a long Sunday, the 6 hour walk with limited water had taken its toll.

There was still a well in the back, the house was still a wreck as if it had been stormed and trashed. There were chairs tipped over, drawers on the ground and chards of broken glass under the broken windows.

"What do you think happened here?" Jack asked.

Thomas responded, "If I had to guess I would say these people said the wrong thing and they paid for it, maybe with their lives. Dale go out and see what the water in the well looks like, hopefully it is drinkable."

As Scott headed out Dale followed. "Dale, I'm going to keep an eye out, while you check the water."

As Dale turned the handle and the bucket of water was being lowered, Scott asked Dale, "I don't want to say it in front of the others, but you seem to worry a lot, don't get me wrong, you are a good soldier, but how do you worry so much without it driving you crazy?"

Dale let out a deep sigh, "I know I worry a lot, my parents hammered into my head that you always look over your shoulder because you never know what the world will throw at you. As if that wasn't bad enough, just as things were settling down and getting a little better the war started, and while other people watched it from a distance, I knew that one day either we would be fighting on its shores or it would be fighting on ours."

The bucket had come up full, looking reasonably good, Dale took a quick smell, he then touched a few drops to his tongue. "It's good, take this is in and I will lower the next bucket in."

Another bucket was on the ground and Scott hit the bottom of it knocking a little bit of dirt out of it. With water but little food they were able to sleep, at least hoping that the next morning would go far better than this one had.

The next morning it was 0600 hours when Thomas woke them all up. "

Everyone, we have a dictator to capture or kill. You have less than 60 minutes to get your gear together and be ready to go, we are not coming back so if you leave anything it's as good as gone."

They all began their walk to the west, April was fast approaching they also knew that the Russians weren't far behind them. Scott began to imagine a radio interview where he was being asked the questions about this story.

He imagined telling them, "It was a long walk we had the Russians not far behind us but we had a mission to do, and when we finally got to Hitler we got him, he was panicking like a guy who was cornered by the cops. I got that knee to his neck and it was the best feeling to take his German rear-end out of there."

He was beginning to imagine the interviewer's praise when his fantasy stopped and he heard Thomas say, "If I had to guess I would say that we have moved about 10 miles since we left Strausberg yesterday, and I think we have walked a mile and a half this morning, with any luck we will get to Berlin before the end of the day."

As they walked they saw a sign at the road that said in German "Altlandsberg 2 km," they knew that was one of the bigger cities, which meant more risk. As they began to walk around the city, a truck with soldiers in it pulled over.

"We have an uprising in Altlandsberg, get in the truck."

Thomas looked at the soldiers, and began speaking in German, "Our truck broke down a few miles ago, let's go."

As they got there they saw the people yelling in German, "Let's have peace," followed by, "No more war."

The soldiers were there with guns drawn, "Get back in your homes, we must control this situation."

Thomas whispered to the guys, "Just follow what these soldiers do, if things get out of control get the hell out."

One of the lieutenants took out a loudspeaker declaring in German,

"Return to your homes, this is a final warning."

As the people yelled back, "Let's have peace, no more war!"

Before Scott fully understood the situation he heard the lieutenant yell, "Feuer!" and they opened fire.

Scott opened fire just a second later than everyone else, and some of them ran as a few more threw things and the lieutenant yelled again, "Feuer!" and they shot again.

He saw the people running back into their homes as he saw the people they had shot lying there in agony on the ground. Dale struggled to keep his composure, at what he had just done, when the German lieutenant came over to Scott and began ranting in German.

"Why did you hesitate? Hesitation is weakness, now is not the time to hesitate!" The German lieutenant walked over and demanded that everyone get back in the truck.

Thomas realizing the serious risk of continuing with this group one by one whispered to the others, "When I give the signal shoot the German soldiers so we can take the truck."

As they got in, the soldiers looked around trying to see who they should shoot when they get the chance, the lieutenant and another soldier were in the front of the truck. Just as Scott was getting into the truck, he saw Rusty coming from behind the other side of the truck. As they waited in stunned silence they all held their guns, looking around at the ones they had to shoot. They waited for the vehicle to stop, then when Thomas gave the signal they all opened fire on the German soldiers. It was sudden chaos, resulting in the death of the other soldiers, it all happened so quickly as the sound of the bullets overwhelmed the senses of all. As they picked off the lieutenant in the front seat and the driver who looked in to find out what was happening.

The noise stopped as everyone looked around seeing that most of them were okay, except Jack had been shot in the upper leg. Dale suddenly ripped the pants off of Jack.

"What are you doing?" Jack asked in a panic.

Dale responded immediately, "I have to get the bullet out and keep pressure on it."

Thomas approvingly said, "Jack don't complain, let Dale do his job, just keep his drawers on. Scott, you and I are going to the front seat, if anyone asks let me do the talking. Michael and Rusty, get the bodies in here and if any of them are still alive put them out of their misery."

As everyone played their role, Scott reluctantly tried to wipe the blood off the seat.

As he finished doing what he could, Thomas said, "That's good enough, get in."

As they sat there driving, Scott looked around wondering if their mission was really close to completion. He turned to Thomas in the driver's seat, "What is the plan?"

Thomas paused, "We drive a decent speed, if anyone asks we are on our way to Berlin with traitors, that way if they see the bodies in the back we have our cover. Once we get to Berlin we find a way to ditch the truck."

Scott paused, "Do you think that will be enough?"

Thomas began to get agitated, "That is the plan, and your job is not to question it. Your job is to execute the plan, are we clear?"

Scott responded, "Yes, sir."

There was another awkward pause, "Look, I know things haven't gone as planned, but you knew what the risks were when you signed up. Besides we already have one worrier back there, we don't need another one, why did you hesitate back there?"

Scott responded, "It took me a second to remember what 'feuer' meant, that's all."

Thomas said, "Well, unless necessary, don't say much, hopefully there will be a few of us left in the end."

As they passed another car, Scott looked out the window turning back to look forward. "Whatever happened to the contact?"

Thomas responded, "The fog of war."

"What?" Scott asked.

"An old phrase; when war happens there are some events and some people that disappear, sometimes for a while, sometimes permanently you can't tell what is going to come out of the fog at you. It's not 20/20, it's blurred and you just do the best you can with what you can."

As the drive went on, they went through checkpoints, the story worked surprisingly well, as they drove closer and closer to Berlin. Even going slowly a mere 12-15 miles an hour they would get the rest of the way to Berlin in an hour and a half. When Dale called to the front they parked the truck, Scott and Thomas went to the back of the truck to examine the situation.

"What's the situation back here?" Thomas asked.

"I've managed to get the bullet out and Jack bit down on a belt to keep his mouth shut, the pressure has reduced the bleeding but if we don't find something to stitch this up with we're in trouble."

Rusty interjected, "We can't leave anyone behind we all know plan D."

Dale turned around in frustration, "How cold hearted are you, this isn't a German, he's one of us, have you forgotten that?"

Thomas wanting to avoid a break down took over the conversation, "Calm down men. Dale, we'll do everything we can, but we can't endanger the mission. Rusty there are only 6 of us and we aren't even in Berlin yet, putting the man out should be a last resort and if anyone is going to pull the trigger it will be the man himself or me. Are we clear?"

They responded, "Yes sir."

"Scott go to the front and see if there is a medical kit under the seats or in the glove-box."

Scott went to the front, seeing the blood and wondering if even stitches could get the job done. He looked under the passenger seat and saw a metal case, as he opened it, the basic medical kit was there. He went to the back of the truck where he was so relieved to say, "I found it."

They made Jack bite down on the belt again as they stitched up his leg and wrapped him in gauze. They sat in the back of the truck as they helped Jack put on another set of pants from one of the dead soldiers. With that issue temporarily resolved they continued the rest of the way to Berlin.

Thomas took a quick look in the rear view mirror and saw the odd car driving by but no one snooping around or any military vehicles approaching.

"Okay men, we're leaving the truck here because the city limits are up ahead, if we take a truck full of dead soldiers into Berlin it will either be the red flag that kills the mission or something that seriously delays the mission in question. Either way, this truck is no longer an asset, it's a liability, not to mention it's almost out of gas anyway."

After they pulled the truck to the side of the road outside the city limits Thomas continued, "If anyone asks, we were on the battlefield near Strausberg, Jack is hurt and we are taking him to the military office to get him examined. Our contact was supposed to help get us in and out of Hitler's building, since we don't have that now, our only hope is precise tactical strikes to sneak in. One more thing, above all else if we do capture Hitler, he has several chests, they look like treasure chests, if we can get him alive, we knock him out, put him in there and we get it out of the building by any means necessary. This may be our last day on earth but if it is, thank God we're going down fighting for freedom and for our country."

Their walk through Berlin was a long one, a city of almost 3 million was bigger than some of them had seen in their lifetimes, Scott's imaginations of glory began to pick up again, while he didn't imagine talking in any significant detail about some of the other parts of this mission, he imagined talking about this part, walking into the lion's den, surrounded by the enemy, literally going right for the enemy, risking it all. He looked over at Dale, who was holding Jack up as Jack was limping. He kept walking but couldn't stop looking at the people who were doing the Hitler salute to them as they came by. It was hard for him to get his head around, he was their enemy, he would be killed if they knew what he was there to do, yet these people saw German soldiers and were saluting them like they were heroes. It was hard for Scott to keep his poker face on and not reveal his confusion and discomfort.

As they walked, a few people in cars asked them where they were going, they stuck to their story of going on their way to the military hospital, Thomas was good at thinking on his feet and when one person asked why he couldn't drive them, he responded, "He needs to keep his leg extended so the muscles don't knot up."

They dodged a few situations that would have sunk the mission, as they got closer and closer to the Nazi headquarters, with the way it had been portrayed Scott felt like they were about to sneak into the Devil's house. This was only accentuated by the giant red banners with the white circled swastikas.

They were getting closer and closer to the building a mere two blocks when they got a clear view of the outside there were roughly 20 guards going back and forth, as they walked around to the sides there were dozens of others as well as four on the roof. They would have a hell of a time getting past that, the daylight was getting away on them. They found an alley not too far away to discuss their new plan.

"What if we wait for nightfall? We are in broad daylight, if they see us we are in deep trouble. Not to mention there is a better chance of Hitler being there."

Thomas looked up at the greying sky, "We are going to need more than nightfall, but at least if we wait a few hours we might come up with something else. We have to be precise, the margin of error has never been tighter."

The sky went dark blue and then became black, the lights around the building didn't help them with visibility as much as they had hoped. Thomas sent Dale, Rusty and Scott into the back of a local bar, since Rusty and Dale were both fluent in German it would be easy for them to pretend to be soldiers raiding the back area to look for Jews. As they approached the back of the bar, Dale put one hand on Scott's shoulder and then on Rusty's.

"Wait a minute," Dale said

Rusty turned around, "What now?"

Dale started, "We are supposed to be looking for Jews, what if there are some in there?"

Scott stopped, "Could we make them part of the mission?"

Rusty whispered angrily, "Are you crazy? Nothing can blow this mission, there are 2 options, victory or death, Hitler goes down no matter what."

Dale and Scott reluctantly went along as they kicked in the back door. In German they declared "Don't move!" as one of the barkeepers was in the back and had dropped a box of whiskey rather suddenly.

Rusty jumped into character, "We were told there were Jews here, hiding with the rest of the rats."

The bartender spoke nervously declaring, "There are no Jews here, Zig Heil!" The salute was one of pure fear. Rusty told Dale and Scott to look around as they looked around in the closets and even in a couple of the barrels. Dale couldn't help but feel dirty, looking for innocent people supposedly to kill them, scaring the living hell out of a barkeeper who is just trying to do his job and support his family and doing it all so they could steal liquor bottles even if it was for a good reason.

They went through and Dale said in German, "It doesn't look like they are here now but, I thought I saw some old sleeves behind one of the barrels, they might have been here before."

The barkeeper scared to death said, "There have never been any Jews here we are loyal to the Fuhrer." This poor scared man played right into their hands.

"The soldiers have been having some tough battles lately, give us some of your bottles and we will know you are loyal to the Fuhrer and to the Fatherland."

The barkeeper absolutely relieved gave in immediately without a moment's thought of the fact he was being stolen from or the lost income, he was just relieved that he would be spared. Scott and Dale both took a case each as Rusty warned the man to keep an eye open. For the first time in days a couple days a plan had gone correctly.

They came back to Thomas who had finished laying out his plan, "Scott, you have done your job well despite not being able to speak German here is where you better pay dividends. Jack is going to pretend to be some lunatic throwing Molotov cocktails near the front gate, as he is yelling like a maniac, the soldiers will try to take him down. Scott this is where you open fire from that roof, pick off every single one of them you can. We are going to be coming in from the back, don't fire at anyone from the back entrance. With any luck the chaos will allow us to slip in pretending to be his security. Jack, this is probably a one way mission, if you get caught, plan D, if you can escape, keep your mouth shut and get to the allied side by any means necessary. Scott, same to you, if you see us escape and can get off the roof without being seen meet up with us. Is everyone clear on the mission?"

They all nodded.

"Men, if I don't make it out of this alive, it's been an honour."

They all took their positions, Scott was the expert marksman, he knew only too well how to pick off soldiers from a distance, he just had to wait for his cue and then send out one well-aimed bullet after another like a machine. He began to wonder if putting Jack in such a vulnerable state barely armed with a bad leg in front of German soldiers was worth it.

Before he could truly think through the implications the fireworks began as Jack yelled like a maniac wreaking havoc in downtown Berlin. He pulled out his gun as the soldiers approached, fired once in the air and then at two of them, suddenly remembering what he had to do. Scott opened fire on the soldiers on the roof and within a matter of 15 seconds all of them had been taken out, as the other soldiers on the ground were looking out trying to see where the shots had come from the soldiers came from the sides as one of them tackled Jack and began beating him. As bad as Scott wanted to help him he had to take out everyone else and keep the Jack diversion in full play.

Several more soldiers were killed before they pinpointed his location. Over half of the guards had been killed, they approached the building, and began to climb to the roof Scott shot the head of the one that poked his head over the top. He fell backward taking out two of the other soldiers that were climbing. Just as Scott began climbing down behind the building he heard another shot ring out. Assuming it was Jack he kept climbing and ran around several other buildings to throw off any potential pursuers.

He finally got a safe distance away he crawled closer to the German head-quarters and saw a few of the soldiers that are left beating Jack. "Where is your ally?"

Scott knew he couldn't help Jack without revealing his location to them and numerous other Nazi soldiers.

Jack said back in German, "Go to hell."

One of the soldiers said, "No you will." They shot him in the back of the head. His head flung back as the bullet left the gun and he fell down on his face. Scott was white-knuckled and knew he had to look out for the soldiers that would now be looking for him. Thankfully the only one that had seen his face was dead. He found a crawlspace under a building to hide for several minutes that allowed him to view the back way into the headquarters. Each minute felt like an eternity, he feared whether his allies would come out at all. He also dreaded having to tell them about Jack's tragic demise.

Finally they came out, he looked and there was nothing that indicated they were carrying a body out, alive or dead. They began to walk away from the building talking their way past the other German soldiers whose numbers had now tripled since the attack several minutes earlier. They all met across town at the rendez-vous point, another ransacked home that they had scoped out across town earlier that day. Scott was left with numerous questions.

Before Scott could get a single word out Thomas spoke up, "Where's Jack?"

Scott responded, "They got to him, he wouldn't give us up so they shot him and his brains came out of his head. So we lost a man for this mission, what happened when you went in there?"

Thomas began to get upset, "Who the hell are you to make demands, I am in command and we lose men all the time this is war. Jack knew the risks."

Before this confrontation could continue Dale spoke up, "Scott calm down, I don't like this either, but we had a major monkey wrench thrown in our mission."

Scott was confused, "What the hell are you talking about?"

Dale who was holding a binder said, "He wasn't in the building, he's not even in the country. The guy who security was rushing off was a double."

Scott's jaw almost fell off, "How do you know that?"

Thomas chimed in, "We saw the group of people leading him away and we heard the double say 'Protect me, or he will hear about this.' We knew something was up right there so we snuck into the room in the name of a security check and we got these books, apparently he left somewhere between eight to ten days ago. Dale, tell him the rest."

Dale took over, "Apparently, he's been planning for this for the last few months since the war has been going so bad for him. The plan says that he has been smuggled out already, he has contacts in Africa who are going to fly him to a transport carrier most of the way across the ocean heading to South America. He's going to lie low there until they reach Argentina, then they are flying to somewhere near the South Pole, it just has co-ordinates that we need to look up."

Rusty looked baffled, "Is he so crazy that he thinks he is going to kill Santa Claus? But forgot that, he would live in the North Pole if he were real?"

Thomas spoke up, "Quiet Rusty, we need all the information we can get. Keep going Dale."

Dale continued, "No he has another bizarre idea, he thinks there is an entirely different species of human somewhere in the centre of the earth."

Dale pulled up a picture of a large hole that seemed to stretch far down.

"Apparently this hole is almost a quarter mile in diameter and he thinks that some super-species of human lives in there and that he can bring them with him to win the war."

Rusty jumped in again, "He's lost his damn mind."

Thomas took over again, "Regardless of how insane he is, our mission isn't over just because he is out of Germany, we have to get him no matter what. I'll chase him to the moon if that is what it takes."

Dale spoke up again, "Not to mention, if there is even a small chance he is right we need to cut him off before he gets there. We can't just say he went into a deep hole and might come out with a new army."

Scott took a deep breath, "I have been through way too much shit since this war started to give up now, let's go get him."

That night they slept in the abandoned house, knowing they would only get a few hours, they had to get out of Germany and chase Hitler to Antarctica or anywhere else they had to. Before going to sleep that night Scott began to daydream about saying he killed Hitler and found these mysterious beings and making them the friends of his country. A war hero and explorer, the women wouldn't be able to resist him, the media would be all over him and he could re-enact what they were doing as part of a Hollywood Movie. Despite everything that had happened that dream allowed him to go to sleep with a smile on his face.

The next morning, Monday March 26, 1945, on just a couple hours of sleep, once again they had to head due west, right to the battlefront and not get killed. In the last few weeks, the allies had gained more ground and were closing in on Berlin. They knew once they got to the allied side they would be fine, just getting there would be life or death. With just 5 men left, Thomas, Scott, Rusty, Dale and Michael, the soldiers set out on their mission.

Rusty tapped Scott on the shoulder, "What is it?" Scott asked.

Rusty responded, "Scott, I don't know if we are going to make it, but if I don't and you do and you get to kill Hitler, tell him my name."

Scott nodded, "Right back at you, but we're going to make it, all of us I can feel it."

Dale who had overheard this looked at him confused, "What makes you think that?"

Scott responded, "We are about to leave Germany, we won't be surrounded by the enemy anymore, we will ambush Hitler in the South Pole, or wherever he is going and then we will return to a hero's welcome."

Dale shook his head, "I wish I could be that optimistic, even if you are right, I don't feel much like a hero."

Thomas had heard enough, "Hey heroes, keep it down back there."

Scott looked at Thomas confused, he couldn't help but think to himself, "Why is he so down on himself? We are risking our lives, we went right into the lion's den, even if we failed we were heroes for trying."

There was an uncomfortable quiet as they walked closer and closer to the western battlefront. Their walk went until noon as their hunger began to impact them, Thomas kept a lookout for an opportunity to speed things up they saw in the distance several trucks driving west.

"Men, wait for this group to pass, look for one or two trucks we can sneak on and make our way to the western battlefront." As the main convoy passed they came closer to the road waiting for more trucks to come by.

Several minutes later one did and stopped asking in German, "Are you on your way to Oppenheim?"

They all nodded and he said, "Then come in, we are going."

They all climbed in the back with several other Nazi soldiers, Scott felt a little uncomfortable, but he knew exactly what he had to do. "Say as little as possible, straight face eyes forward."

However his eyes occasionally wandered and he saw one soldier who suddenly burst into tears, their commander turned to him and began berating him, "Are you crying about your brother again, what are you a woman? He is dead, it is war take that anger put it in your hands and fire it at those Americans."

The man was not comforted and continued to bawl, the commanding officer grabbed him by the collar and began slap him in the face repeatedly.

"What's the matter with you, you are a soldier, you do not show weakness! If the Americans could see you now they would laugh at you for crying like a little girl. Be a soldier!"

Scott was stunned, he had been told to man up before, but if his brother had been old enough to enroll and had been killed he would have gotten more sympathy, at least an "I'm sorry for your loss" or a "I know it's tough." He was looking at the enemy, someone he might have to kill very soon, but for the first time he actually felt sympathy for one of these men wearing the other uniform. At the same time he was relieved that it distracted them from questioning him or any of his crew of spy soldiers.

They drove for a few hours with little if anything being said, the tension had been slowly building as the other soldiers were getting more white-knuckled about what they were about to face. Scott could see the wheels turning in Dale's mind, before they had gotten in the truck he had hid the one inch binder in the back of his uniform so that suspicion wouldn't be raised.

Scott began to wonder what Dale was thinking about, what was he worrying about now?

The commander began speaking in German, "When you get to the field, it is very simple, stop them from gaining another inch. If they take an inch you make them pay for it with blood, after everything we have been through we are not going to give up now."

The soldiers became excited, however the one who had wept looked despondent and the commander began to fume. "What is wrong with you, we are Germans we are the master race we will win for the Fuhrer Zeig Heil!"

That soldier looked up his mood changed entirely and stared a hole through him as the commander asked, "Why are you looking at me like that for?"

Scott looked at Thomas for direction as he gave the look that said, "Any second now."

The soldier stood up as his eyes burned with fire as he said, "I'm the only one left, my father died three years ago, my brother is dead, if I die who will look after my mother?"

The commander shoved him back down, "Fall in line, the fatherland comes before all else. If you die fighting the enemy then it's worth it!"

The soldier finally lost it, he stood up and shot the commander, the shot threw the commander backwards onto Dale and Thomas and they had to shove him off as the other German soldiers leapt on him. Thomas snapped his fingers as Dale, Michael, Rusty, Scott and Thomas opened fire on the eight soldiers that had leapt on the other German soldier. The bullets rang out and only a couple of the German soldiers were able to fire any shots, as the bullets went off Michael went down as they finished killing the other soldiers. The soldier who had shot his commander began to crawl up from the bodies holding his arm that had been shot.

The truck came to a stop as the driver came around to see what had happened, Scott aimed the bullet right between his eyes and killed him. As Thomas checked on Michael, Rusty and Thomas pulled the other soldier out and Rusty pushed him up against the wall of the inside of the truck.

Rusty spoke in German, "Look you Nazi tell us how to get across or we will blow your damn brains out."

With a shocked look on his face he blurted out, "Traitors?"

Dale leapt in, "Rusty, back off he has been through enough."

The German soldier said, "American."

Dale began in German, "What's your name?"

The soldier responded, "I am Ludvig, my mother named me after Beethoven the legendary composer."

Dale said, "You stood up to them because you want to protect your mother?"

Ludvig responded, "Yes, if I die, she will have no one."

Dale responded, "Look, if you help us get across safely to the allies, we will tell them you helped us and they will keep you safe until the war is over and you will be able to help your mother."

Ludvig struggled for a moment, his internal conflict was clear to everyone. "Okay, I will help you, you did save me."

Rusty chimed in English, "One of our own got shot in the process."

Thomas raised his finger silencing Rusty then he began to speak to Ludvig, "Do we have a deal?"

Ludvig extended his left hand since he had been shot in the right elbow. Scott watched all of this, hoping that this would work. Thomas once again took the wheel of the truck, Scott and Rusty watched Ludvig and helped him apply basic medical tape and Dale was trying to help Michael. Dale's medical training was coming in handy yet again.

Rusty whispered in Scott's ear, "You are the best shot of all of us, if he tries anything, blow his damn head off."

Scott looked back at Ludvig with suspicion, but couldn't help but wonder, "Why was Rusty still so suspicious?"

Several minutes later they pulled off the battlefield and just over the hill the allies were coming straight for them. Inside the benches in the truck were extra supplies, including replacement shirts, which could be turned into white flags. Ludvig told them how to use the radio to contact the allies along with the road that they were told to stay off of. As they approached waving the white flags, numerous British soldiers with their guns drawn surrounded the truck. They declared with their English accent filling the air, "Come out with your hands up, don't try anything or we will open fire."

Thomas spoke to them after they got back to their base telling them that they were Americans with the exception of Ludvig. One of the British soldiers snickered, "They sound like Americans alright."

He didn't go into any detail but he did tell them they had been on a confidential spy mission and corresponding with General Hondo on the American side would verify this. Due to the circumstances they were suspicious but were willing to investigate. Dale said farewell to Ludvig, he gave Ludvig a hug saying, "Take care of your family."

Ludvig was stunned by his showing of compassion he responded, "Thank you sir."

Dale walked away feeling confident that things would turn out okay for Ludvig as he had finally done the right thing. There was some tension over the binder that Dale had been carrying with him, the soldiers looked it over to ensure it had no weapons but left it with them on the command of their lieutenant. Hours went by as the waiting went on and on, waiting for who knows how many people to get back to them to verify this story. It was 4 pm the next day when they called Thomas up, "Thomas, your General Hondo is on the line and he wants to speak to you."

Everyone else left the room except for lieutenant who was armed with a rifle. Scott watched carefully hoping that they could finally come out from being prisoners. Dale spoke to Scott, "I know I should be patient, but we have a limited window here, and depending on where the ship was when Hitler was dropped off he might be in Antarctica already. If we are lucky he is still on his way to Argentina and we can catch him before he gets to Antarctica."

Scott looked at him, "You don't buy into this hollow earth thing do you?"

Dale responded, "I know that it's probably ridiculous but there is a small chance. Besides, this war has to end."

Scott asked him, "How come yesterday you said you didn't feel like a hero?"

Dale responded, "We have had to do some things that I'm not proud of, that was why I wanted to show Ludvig some mercy. After some of the things we have done on this mission, when I have to face St. Peter at the pearly gates, I don't know how I will explain myself."

Scott hadn't thought of it that way, he always drew a line between his actions as himself and his actions as the soldier. Before Scott could think about that any further, Thomas came out and said, "Gentlemen, join me in this room we need to discuss the next part of the mission. Dale bring the binder, right now." Scott, Dale and Rusty joined Thomas in the room as the British Lieutenant left.

General Hondo began, "Okay so where is he going, how is he going to get there and where can we get the drop on him?"

Thomas nodded at Dale indicating it was his turn to speak, "We don't know where he is on the path but what we can say is that he left their base in Northern Africa flew out into the ocean to meet with a German ship via radio, the ship has been out on the water since January, as a contingency plan. They are meeting with their allies in Argentina who will or already have set up a plane for them to go to Antarctica. The worst case scenario is that he is already there, the best case scenario is that the ship hasn't reached Argentina yet."

The General followed up, "So what do you need?"

Thomas stepped in, "We need a couple of direct flights there, we just need somewhere in Antarctica to land that will be close to them."

General Hondo paused, "Okay, hold tight, I will make as many calls as I have to get you there. According to the Brits Lieutenant Oliver, Michael was hit in a bad spot and even though he will probably recover he is out of the picture and since the other 3 are gone, it's down to the 4 of you. Thomas, Scott, Dale, Rusty, the four of you are going to finish this, I can't stress enough how important this is, we will get you to there, money is no object, catch or kill him and I will owe you all a drink when you get back."

Thomas responded, "Thank you sir."

The call ended as the question was not if they would find Hitler but when and what would happen when they finally got to him. The next two days went by very slowly as they did general cleaning duties and other non-combative roles waiting for their ship to come in. Rusty's impatience was getting the better of him, "How long does it take? We are at war, the enemy is getting further and further away and we are just here cleaning toilets and mopping up for the British. I thought we threw their tea into the Boston Harbour so we wouldn't have to do this."

Thomas had heard enough, "Shut it Rusty, history aside the British are our allies now, they are working with us to end this war and as we are all taught when we enter the service, every job no matter how big or how small is for doing."

Rusty's resentment was clear despite the fact that he said nothing in response. At 7 pm on Thursday March 29, the call they had waited for with such urgency had come through from General Hondo's assistant. "At 0500 hours tomorrow, you will be picked up and we have two more flights waiting for you. Get your sleep on the plane because as soon as you arrive at our base you will be expected to put on your winter gear and head over to their location. We expect you to land in Antarctica by Saturday roughly noon, there will be another plane picking you up Monday morning so you will have less than 48 hours to get in there, get him and get out".

The next morning they all got into the planes, with one long flight after another, Scott began to daydream thinking about getting there to Antarctica and the moment when the four of them had Hitler cornered and they can fly him back to the states to put him on trial. He could just imagine his face on the front cover of the newspaper and the hero's welcome he would get when he went back home.

At one point Thomas sat down next to him and said, "Scott I need to talk to you for a moment while the other two are asleep."

Scott nodded his head and quietly responded, "Okay."

Thomas continued, "Rusty is too eager and Dale is a little too hesitant and a worrier. You are the most level headed of the three left under my command I need to know, what are you going to do when we get there?"

Scott answered simply, "Finish the mission, capture Hitler, and if he can't be captured kill him and bring back the body."

A modest grin came across Thomas' face, "Good, I just want to make sure you haven't lost sight of what is important here. It's going to be damn cold down there, but it won't be nearly as cold as the reception we will get if we have to tell them that we let him slip through our fingers and that he is still running loose. You're a good man Scott, I know you will do the right thing."

With that Scott let his eyes close, knowing he had a long two days ahead of him chasing down the most dangerous man on earth, knowing that the choice to pull the trigger might be his, knowing it might be him that determines whether this mission succeeds or fails. All of that pressure by itself made him tired but still unable to sleep.

The pilot announced, "We will be landing in 30 minutes, please prepare everything so that nothing is left behind." They had been given a change of uniforms and they all changed facing the wall into them, this time there was no point in pretending to German soldiers any longer, they put on their American uniforms and prepared for the final confrontation. Rusty finished putting his suit on first Scott looked over his shoulder to see Rusty packing his bag.

As everyone finished theirs in the last minute Rusty looked at all of them, "Guys, victory or death."

Dale turned to Thomas, "Do we have reinforcements coming?"

Thomas paused, "This is a covert mission, we can't endanger it by involving too many people. The last I heard they were looking over potential candidates. Even so, by the time they get approved and shipped over here, it would be days, the people at the base are security, not soldiers they might help us get ready but the bottom line is when we get out there it is the 4 of us." Scott could plainly see the concern on Dale's face Dale probably had five different bad scenarios running through his head one after another.

They arrived at the base where they were told about a radio interception that said the plane from Argentina would be arriving in a matter of hours. They looked at the maps and the pictures from the binder; Scott, Dale and Rusty stood a couple steps back as Thomas conversed with Captain Troy.

"So we are about 60 miles away from the Argentinian base that Hitler is being sent to?"

Troy responded, "Yes and based on your co-ordinates the place where they will be headed is over this ridge and is about 52 miles from here and 15 miles from where they are."

Thomas continued, so if they are landing soon they may be heading there shortly after landing, if so we walk straight to the hole we might be able to catch them by surprise."

The captain chuckled, "In this terrain, going that far you better have something better than your feet."

Thomas looked at him confused, "We have walked a long way before, we marched across a war zone."

Troy responded, "True, but when it's this cold out all the time and the snow you step in grips and makes every step twice as hard as it normally is you will run out of energy quickly, which is the last thing you want if you are going to fight. Let me loan you some dog sleds, it will take a few hours but it will save your energy and trust me you will need it."

They packed their weapons, their maps and their heavy jackets, just before they left there was another intercepted radio message, "They have just arrived and they are in a hurry to get out on the ice, there are about 20 men."

Thomas looked at the men, with a renewed concern, "We don't have numbers or stealth, no one has the home field advantage, all we have left is the element of surprise and boatload of determination."

Dale and Scott got into one dog sled manned by one of the bases men as Thomas and Rusty got into the other. The two dog sleds moved quickly, these huskies had done this before and moved like a well-oiled machine. There was the occasional bump as they continued across the white landscape, Scott felt a minor bit of joy from it like a toboggan ride when he was a child.

They stopped to take a couple of breaks to the frustration of Rusty, "How do people live in this crappy place, I'm from Florida, I want to get this over with." Thomas repeatedly scolded him for his lack respect for the people helping them across this cold barren land.

Finally, they reached the point that their map said they should stop, a mile and a half away from the quarter mile hole. They could see it from the distance, Scott couldn't help but comment, "Damn, I know the picture said a quarter mile, but that is huge."

The dog sled drivers let them out, "We will be back in an hour, keep your compass and keep your wits about you."

The soldiers walked for almost 20 minutes looking around for any sign of Hitler's group, suddenly Rusty saw one.

"There they are," he opened fire missing that soldier and drawing fire from a few others with barely anywhere to run except down the hill behind them.

Thomas was livid, "What the hell are you doing you damn fool you almost got us killed!" Before they could think of their next move, they were surrounded by almost a dozen Nazi soldiers.

Rusty was burning with outrage as they walked him back towards Hitler emerging from behind several other men, asking in German, "What is this, who are these men?"

One of the German soldiers said, "They are Americans who came to attack us."

Hitler shook his head and began to speak in imperfect English, "No one is going to stop the glory of Germany, you threw your lives away coming here."

He turned around and began to walk away when he said in German, "Kill them."

Before the soldiers could cock their guns Rusty yelled out, "Victory or death!" as he threw a grenade with a pulled pin in the air. Scott immediately leapt away unsure of how it would land and who would be left standing.

It all happened so quickly numerous soldiers were running Hitler away with Hitler yelling in German, "To the hole, that's why we are here." Remaining soldiers were either dead or on the ground a shot went off and a gun was tossed next to Scott where he opened fire on the soldiers who were beginning to get back up. The last few were killed as Scott and Dale reached their feet seeing Rusty blown apart and seeing Thomas with his legs having been blown off at the knees and his front badly burned gasping next to a dead Nazi.

Dale ran over, "Thomas we can get you back."

Thomas grabbed him by the throat as he leaned in, "Forget me, take that son of a bitch out, now!"

Dale and Scott looked at each other and followed the footprints that had been made just a minute earlier by Hitler's men.

Scott and Dale picked up their guns made sure they had some bullets and began the chase, suddenly that cold air seemed to disappear, the explosions and pressure had made an ice cold day irrelevant. The adrenaline flowed through their bodies, their breath in the air was like smoke coming out of a fire breathing dragon. After almost two minutes of running they had the German group in sight, much of the way to the quarter mile hole, they had slowed to a walk. Scott and Dale looked at each other knowing what the other was thinking. Scott and Dale laid low and pulled out their rifles and began aiming at the crowd and Scott began picking them off with head-shot after head-shot. After the first four they turned around trying to fire back however they were losing people fast. Hitler began to scream as five of them charged as Hitler and three other continued on.

The distance was too much, before Hitler's men could reach them, Dale and Scott had killed them all. Unfortunately the uphill that was heading back down put Hitler and his people once again out of reach as Dale and Scott got back up to continue the pursuit. Dale grabbed one of the guns one of the Germans were carrying, hoping it would still have ammunition in it. Hitler and his men were about half a football field away from the quarter mile hole when Dale and Scott caught up and once again and went to fire, unfortunately Dale's first gun was empty and just as he went to fire the German gun he had picked up he was shot at the same time and went down.

Scott managed to shoot the others but he was now out of bullets with Hitler being alone. All he had left was his bare hands but he was going to go after him, he was going to do whatever it took to finish the mission. He finally caught Hitler about 40 yards from the quarter mile hole as they began throwing punches back and forth.

He tried to tackle Hitler to the ground but Hitler had turned it around into a choke from behind, Scott took one more deep breath and flipped Hitler forward and began to punch him as he was on the ground, Hitler kicked back hitting Scott in the face breaking his nose. Hitler attempted to run past him back to where the bodies of his fallen protectors were with a gun on the ground. Scott leapt up and tackled Hitler just as he was reaching down to pick it up, they exchanged more punches, with every punch that Scott connected the harder he wanted to throw the next one.

Finally as Hitler went to pick up a gun, his hand was kicked and the gun flew several feet back as the chase was on again, they brawled and rolled ever closer to the gun that would end this battle. They got back up as Scott suddenly felt an even bigger rush of energy and rage and declared his judgment with each new punch, "This is for the people you killed, this is for the soldiers, this is for my friends."

As Hitler fell backward clutching his body and face, Scott threw one more punt kick hitting Hitler in the jaw leaving him briefly dazed on the ground. "That's for me."

Scott went back and picked up the gun they had been fighting over and there he walked closer, cocked the gun and aimed it as he had aimed so many guns the previous few years. "This is for the future." He fired the gun, it hit its target exactly as planned, he let his arm fall the gun hitting the snow finally feeling the physical pain, finally feeling the cold but also feeling relief that it was over.

He walked over to the quarter mile hole, seeing if there was anything down there but all he saw was a chasm of darkness. He looked back to where Dale was and began to walk to make sure he was okay. As he finally reached him, Dale explained that he had been hit in the side of the leg and that with a little help he could walk. As they walked back, to where Thomas had been they came back to see the small massacre and Dale went over to take Thomas' pulse.

"He's dead." With everything else weighing on them they now had yet another death.

Scott and Dale continued the walk back to where the dog sled would be waiting for them, the several minutes that followed felt like an eternity as the wind got colder and the snowfall had begun and got heavier.

Scott mentioned to Dale, "When we get back I may need you to verify that I did kill Hitler and you saw it."

Dale said, "Don't worry I will, you will need all the proof you can get."

Scott confused asked, "What do you mean?"

Dale answered, "The weather in the southern hemisphere is the opposite of the northern hemisphere, they have summer when we have winter and vice versa. With the way the snow is coming down and how hard it is to get here and how deep the snow is in the winters here, he might get buried so deep no one will ever find him."

Scott was bothered by this but tried to improve things, "Well, at least it's finally over and the Fuhrer is dead."

They saw the dog sled and after getting additional blankets put on them and they settled in for the trip back Dale said in passing said, "After everything we've been through, it doesn't feel right, you expect something better than a long walk through the middle of nowhere."

Scott began, "Yeah, after everything we have been through…."

Suddenly a rush of flashing memories: what he had seen the soldiers doing what they were told, the bartenders not standing up for themselves, even the children following along with the Nazi salute never being allowed to question anything. He suddenly realized all of it was still there, the next day the war would still be going on, the armies would still be unrelenting and harsh and they still wouldn't know what happened to their contact.

Before they reached the base Scott zoned out, the judging eyes of the dead body from Bergen Belsen were staring a hole through him. The sled driver as they were approaching the base said, "When you announce that you killed Hitler you are going to get a hero's reception in there".

Dale said, "I don't know if I can handle that."

The sled driver was very confused, "Why not?"

Scott closed by saying, "Because all we did was kill a few men. We haven't won what really matters."

THE FOOL

One day two boys came home from school, they were waiting for a phone call. Matt and Jason, they were in 8th grade and were waiting with unease, Jason began to pace.

"Do you think it will work?"

Matt responded, "Of course it will, that A is as good as ours. What game do you want to play?"

Matt's grandfather came in, and said, "Hello," and asked, "Where are Mom and Dad?"

Matt responded, "Mom is picking Natalie up from the mall, and Dad is working late and will be home around 8."

Grandpa began, "I was told your sink in the basement was clogged, I'll be down there fixing it, if you need anything."

Matt responded, "Okay Grandpa, I will."

As the basement door closed Jason began to get even more worried, "Great; if he finds out, we're busted."

Matt said, "Stop worrying, he's downstairs and his hearing probably isn't that good anyway."

Finally the phone rang and they saw it was Kimberly. Their grandfather came back from the basement as they picked up.

"Yeah, he bought it, that fish-faced geek really thinks you'll be his girlfriend if he does the whole new project. That is fantastic, the only thing better than that A is going to be that look on his face, when he gets a dose of reality. Yeah, see you at the party on Friday, bye Kim."

Matt turned to Jason, "See that sucker is going to do all the work, we get an A and a good laugh, it's all good."

The grandfather came out from behind the doorway having heard enough.

"The hell it is, what the hell is wrong with you, taking advantage of people!"

Jason began to stutter, "W-we were, weren't doing an-anything!"

Matt turned to Jason in annoyance, "Look Gramps, we're just teaching a kid an important life lesson: don't be a fool." He let out a chuckle, as Jason became even more nervous about what would happen next.

Jason began to walk towards the door saying, "Bye Matt, see you at school tomorrow."

The grandfather grabbed him by the arm and said, "Where do you think you're going, get back over there."

Jason went back to where he was as the grandfather let out a disappointed sigh, saying, "Well Matt, I've got a life lesson for you, you think he's the fool, maybe he is, but the biggest fool is you."

Matt looked at him confused, "What are you talking about?"

The grandfather responded, "I've been around long enough to know that people are so damned short sighted, they don't realize that every time you take advantage of someone you destroy trust and make people more afraid to be generous, which is something the world needs plenty more of."

Matt said, "Why are you bringing the world into this? This is between us, so be quiet, don't tell anyone and just let me get that A."

The grandfather passed and said, "Fine give me $50 and I keep my mouth shut."

Matt asked, "$50?"

The grandfather said, "That's my price."

Jason looked at Matt and said, "Dude, he'll tell."

Matt said, "Fine, the day of."

The grandfather spoke up. "No, in advance."

Matt said, "I can't do that, we don't have that much on us."

The grandfather said, "Fine half now, half the day of."

Matt looked annoyed but said, "Okay, but you better keep quiet."

A few weeks went by, as things went according to plan, and the day came. As Matt was getting ready for school, he was so happy that everything was going according to plan, his mother said, "Matt, I have to run some errands so your grandfather is taking you to school today."

Matt tried to pass it off as no big deal, but inside he was so nervous as his grandfather drove him to school, he mentioned that he wanted the other $25, and Matt gave it to him, as he was relieved that the tension that had haunted him was almost over. His history class was second period as he told Kimberly to tell Gerald at the end of the day, that he was getting nothing.

He couldn't wait, Gerald handing in the assignment as Jason said, "Matt you genius, you did it."

A few minutes later the teacher came to the front of the class and began speaking. "I'm glad everyone handed in their assignment on time, I have decided to do something different this year, I'm going to have a group present their report in front of the class." She paused for a moment, "Group 3 why don't you come on up?"

Matt began to panic, "Mrs. Waller we weren't prepared for a presentation."

She responded, "Just talk for 10 minutes about what you learned about colonial North America's history."

Matt was trying not to panic, as he got up to the front of the class with Jason and Kimberly, they looked at Gerald, "Gerald come up."

Gerald looked at them with disgust as he moved his thumb across this throat, mouthing the words, "You're dead."

The teacher spoke up and said, "Gerald isn't good at public speaking so the 3 of you will."

The teacher went to the back of the class as Jason began to speak with dread, "Early colonial times were interesting, they...they didn't have technology, but, they…. Had spirit, yeah."

As Jason stumbled over his words, Matt looked at Gerald, who mouthed the words, "I know."

Matt looked at this teacher who held up $25 with a scowl on her face, then the classroom door quietly opened and his grandfather poked his head in held up his $25 and with a big mischievous smile he pointed and whispered the word, "Gotcha".

Matt felt worse than he ever had in his life; he had been double crossed by his teacher and his grandfather. He knew that an F, detention and more awaited him, Jason, and Kimberly. However, he realized that F was well earned for a fool like him.

ALTERNATE ENDING

Chad came home to his apartment, with his head down, defeated; it was five months since he had worked more than a week here and there. He and his girlfriend Maryse's savings were absolutely depleted and it was made that much worse when he was given a note by the building manager. He read the note as he came through the door; the note said he had one week to come up with the rent before he and Maryse would be evicted. Maryse was going to school full time and her part time job barely paid for her textbooks and a few groceries. His eyes began to well up with tears, wondering what he was going to do.

He sat there on the couch and checked his e-mail once again, getting no responses from the jobs he applied for online. As he began to weep Maryse came through the door and sat down next to him holding him saying, "It will be okay, we will get through this. I know you will think of something."

Through his tears he said, "No it won't, we'll be evicted in 5 days. Even if I get a job I won't get paid until it's too late."

Maryse stared at the notice in disbelief wondering what they would do next, her own heart raced as she realized what dangerous situation they were really in. That night they watched TV and tried to hold each other, Chad held on even tighter believing she was all he had left.

The next day he saw that they were hiring for a bartender down in the city. He went down there only to discover that the job had already been taken by a woman with ample cleavage. He sat down at the table and stared out the window, looking absolutely lost. He happened to look over at the next table and see two guys who were asking about seeing "Bones Malone" for some cash.

Chad reluctantly went over and asked them about Bones Malone and they first said, "Are you a cop?"

He said, "No."

They responded, "Bones Malone gets you cash quick if you need it, but you better pay him back, because your bones are his collateral."

Chad looked outside at the falling snow, realizing that he and his girlfriend would be outside in the cold if he didn't. So he asked them to give him the directions to find Bones Malone.

Chad got there and two guys frisked him to make sure he didn't have any weapons or microphones. He approached Bones Malone, he was a tough looking man with reflective sunglasses who was in his 50's. He had some old marks on his face from what had probably been a hard life. Chad told Bones what was happening and Bones interrupted him part way, "Look Chad, I don't need your life story, I just need to know how much and when you are paying it back?"

Chad took a deep breath and said, "We need about $4,000 to cover the last three months of rent, and to help pay next month's while I try to find a job."

Bones asked him, "Do you have anything lined up?"

Chad looked at him and said, "Not yet, but I am trying every day and I can't stand the thought of my girlfriend and myself being put out on the street."

Bones interrupted him, "Don't get so emotional, I'll help you out, but I got a few terms. First, I charge 15% interest per week, compounded weekly. Second, you have six weeks to start paying me back, you better not leave town, because you don't want me and my guys to come and get you."

A lump the size of a golf ball formed in Chad's throat and he said, "Okay, we'll do it."

They shook hands and he was given the money, he was relieved and frightened at the same time. As the next few weeks went by, he kept looking and looking for a job, he had a phone interview, but they didn't call back.

What was tearing him apart inside was the thought of Bones Malone and his cronies walking into his apartment and hurting him but more importantly Maryse, he couldn't bear the thought of it. After about three weeks, he heard a knock at the door, he wasn't sure who it was since Maryse was at school. He opened the door to see it was Bones Malone and his friends.

Chad was stunned, frightened to death of why he was here, and he could barely gain enough composure to say, "Bones, how are you I remember having six weeks and it has only been three."

Bones told his cronies, "Go look around."

Chad began to panic, "For what?"

Bones said, "Look, standard procedure, we come in every once in a while to make sure you're still here and that you aren't planning on going anywhere with our money."

Chad took a deep breath to try and calm down, "We aren't going anywhere I am still applying for jobs and I'm waiting to hear back from a guy who I had a phone interview with yesterday."

Bones stared right in his eyes, "I've seen that look before."

Chad looked puzzled, "What look?"

Bones said, "The look of an honest but desperate man. You better hope you get that job or something else soon. Most of all don't leave town. Got it?" Bones menacingly pointed at him as he said that.

One of his cronies came back to the door, "Nothing is packed."

Bones responded as he turned to leave, "Good, and Chad, it better stay that way, because we will be checking in every now and then."

A few more days went by as his other attempts seemed to fall through and his new month of rent was due, Maryse had noticed how sad, tense and riddled with anxiety he had become. He hadn't told her he went to a loan shark, he told her that he went to work out a deal with the landlord. She asked him what was wrong, he tried to brush it off but she saw through it, when he finally told her, everything.

He told her about the loan shark, the threats and the periodic visits he saw the fear and anger in her face as she leapt to her feet, "You lied to me, now we might die!"

Chad was overcome with regret, "Look Maryse, I'm sorry, I'm so sorry, I would do anything to be able to provide for you and get us out of this. I mean it, anything."

The next few weeks went by as the struggle continued. Two interviews went nowhere and the six week deadline was approaching. Chad reluctantly told Maryse that they will need to leave town the instant she finishes the school year because if they don't he is scared of what would happen to her. She reluctantly agreed, knowing the corner they had been painted into, she had repeatedly told Chad that she trusted him to solve their financial problems.

With just a few days left Maryse came home from school to find that Bones Malone was there and his goons were holding Chad.

"Listen up Chad, I don't care where you get the money, I don't care if your mother dies, whether you rob a liquor store but you had better give me some of the $9,252 you owe me."

Maryse enraged blurted out, "What the hell are you talking about we borrowed $4,000?"

Bones turned to her, "Interest is 15% per week, compounded weekly, I told your boyfriend this when he borrowed it. You know Chad we might call this deal even if you send your girl here to work for me, I'm sure she would bring in some money looking like that."

Maryse balled up her fist, "You son of a bitch."

When his bodyguard pulled his gun, "Don't even think about it peaches."

Maryse stomped into her room as Bones gestured to his men to leave, "Get me that money by Saturday Chad, and if I were you I would put that girl of yours in her place."

As they left Chad was overwhelmed with the feeling of failure, he had failed to provide, he had failed to protect her and he failed to defend her honour. He felt like a complete failure as a man. In a last desperate act he tried to call the witness Protection Program but there was a waiting list for available places, with only three days remaining that wasn't an option.

Late that night, he packed everything that they would need and removed anything that could give Bones or his men a chance to track them. Her last exam was on the Thursday and he made the decision that they would leave the town, the province and the country if they had to. The next day he got on the bus with two suitcases to meet her at the school, little did he realize someone was parked on the street outside his building, had seen him and had called Bones Malone.

As planned she finished her exam and left for the parking lot, but as she approached it she saw Bones Malone and one of his men waiting in front of her car with a flat tire.

"Going somewhere?"

Her eyes lit up realizing what was happening and that the bus stop at her school was letting Chad out at the worst time.

Maryse yelled, "Chad run!"

They both ran for the school, as Bones Malone and his henchman split up to chase after them. Bones Malone chased after Maryse, not realizing she was a distance runner. Chad was losing ground to Bones' large henchman because he was carrying two suitcases so he threw one down, tripping him and continued running towards the school's Building D entrance. Maryse kept running as Bones began to get winded and Chad's heart was pounding as he was beginning to lose ground again.

He took a left through the tunnel that he knew would lead him to building C where Maryse had re-entered. Bones' henchmen was being slowed by down by the people he was trying to dodge. As Chad left the tunnel he raced down to the first floor where he looked for Maryse but with no luck. He ran towards the janitor's closet, hoping he could figure out his next move. As he closed the door behind him, he looked around absolutely stunned and speechless.

He was suddenly on a darkened movie set, over a few dozen feet to his left he saw a single spotlight over a director's chair. He was drawn to it and as he got closer he saw a manuscript with a blue cover and a pen on it. His curiosity pulled him to it like a magnet. He opened the script and saw everything that had happened and was happening in his life, reminding him of his failure. When he turned to the last few pages he was horrified.

According to the script he was supposed to text Maryse that they should double back to the car, grab everything and take the bus out of town. While they were at the car, Bones and his henchmen would catch them, take them at gunpoint to their car. They would then beat him, shoot him in the head and sell Maryse to human traffickers. The last scene describes the abuse she suffers crying for help with no one hearing it as it all fades to black. Tears flowed out of his eyes as he couldn't bear the thought of that happening to her.

He looked at the small table next to the director's chair and saw a clock that said 12:48 along with a standing card that said, "Filming continues at one o'clock."

Chad knew he had to do something, he picked up the pen and began crossing out what was there and tried to write something else. He started with writing, "Bones decided to give up on crime, went home and never bothered Chad and Maryse again."

Suddenly what he wrote was highlighted in orange and disappeared. He began to panic when he wrote, "Chad suddenly gained superpowers leapt into the air, snatched Bones and his goon and dropped them in jail."

This time it was highlighted in red and disappeared. He suddenly looked at the top of the script and saw a legend with a few colours listed and next to red it said "impossible" and next to orange it said "inconsistency/plothole." Suddenly he looked at the clock, which now said 12:51 realizing he now had less than 9 minutes to write an ending to save Maryse.

He remembered something Maryse had said once, "Creativity isn't forced, it flows." He took a deep breath and wrote something else, hoping this would save Maryse.

As the alarm hit one, he had written what he could and suddenly he was transported back into the janitor's closet with no memory of what had just happened. Chad texted Maryse telling her to stay on the 4th floor and to call the police immediately, he put on the jacket in the suitcase he still had, he came out of the janitor's closet as he began to walk towards the parking lot. Bones and his henchmen were walking by as they saw him walking toward the car.

Just as they were running towards him he turned holding his chest from stress pain which they thought was a gun and they opened fire. He fell backward to the shock of all the onlookers, who began to panic and a few pulled out their camera phones. Bones realizing he was exposed told his henchmen they had to leave right now. Maryse witnessed all of this happening while she was left on the 4th floor, the sight of Chad ripped her heart out, she had never felt more helpless or devastated than at that moment.

Due to the surveillance footage, Maryse's testimony, and numerous witnesses, Bones was put away for life and his colleagues were also put away for many, many years. Despite this victory, Maryse did not feel like she had won anything, all she felt was loss. Her classmates put together a Kickstarter for her to help her make it through her 4th year of school, but the loss continued to haunt her.

Despite graduating she had a hard time finding a job in her field after a year, and gave up on the advice of her new boyfriend Arnie. Arnie had been putting her down for a while and now she was working an exploitative restaurant called Jugs & Mugs, getting catcalls rather than being a director making the calls. She had reached the point of believing she couldn't do any better, after one fatefully bad day she decided that this was it, this was her life and she couldn't take it anymore. As she tied up the last of her loose ends she walked into her apartment and planned on taking an overdose of pills. But just before she was about to, she stopped to double check the closet in her bedroom, thinking perhaps she could find something fancier to die in, when she walked onto a set just like the one Chad had walked onto.

She was drawn to the director's chair with a single spotlight over it. As she approached she saw a small table right next to it, with a script with a blue cover, she opened it and saw the events that had happened a few years ago but saw the part that had been changed. She immediately recognized Chad's handwriting, she read through the script and read through the parts he had crossed out and she was stunned at what she had been saved from. His writing reminded her of the love notes he sometimes left on the fridge in the morning, and she began to reminisce about the other things he used to do and how great she felt when she was with him.

She came back to this unusual reality, she then looked at the script that was on the director's chair itself with a pen and a green cover, she read through it and she saw the script called for her to kill herself and for the screen to go to black as Arnie sarcastically and callously said, "Great, just great, the police are going to think this is my fault."

She looked at the first script and saw that something had been changed to save her; she realized that if she committed suicide then Chad's sacrifice would have been for nothing. She picked up the scripts and went for the door to discover that something prevented them from leaving this realm. At a certain point it seemed like an incredibly strong hand kept them from moving another inch. However she pulled and pulled the pen fell to the floor and rolled partially under the door. She re-wrote a better ending, one where she breaks up with Arnie, packs up her things and finds something better. Just to make sure another tragedy wouldn't be written by anyone else she took the pen with her.

THE TALE OF PRINCE EVERETT

It was the 1400's in England when Prince Everett stepped onto the balcony. He took a deep breath, observing a piece of the kingdom that he believed would one day be his. He heard that far away, roughly two days travel by horseback, was a large forest where people were scared to tread. The legend had it that a witch lived in the forest that everyone was scared of. The reason why this concerned the King was that the witch was not paying taxes and had not pledged allegiance to the royal crown.

One night around the dinner table the King was talking about how he would deal with this witch if he only had time. The captain of the guards explained that he didn't want to leave the area because he'd heard rumours of French aggression. Prince Everett saw this as an opportunity, the first of many in his ultimate goal. Everett spoke up and proudly proclaimed that he would have this witch.

"Waving our flag, or she will be one dead hag!"

All the men raised their glasses and cheered as Everett revelled in their praise.

The next morning Everett assembled five guards to accompany him: Oswald, Edmund, Louis, Matthew, and his most loyal guard Reginald who had watched over him since he was a boy. Before they left the castle Reginald told Everett, "I applaud you sir, all I beseech is that you be cautious. If you were lost on this journey your father would put my head on a spike."

Everett chuckled, "Fear not, good Reginald, no witch is a match for the royal guard."

Edmund spoke up nervously, "What if there are more, a coven of Satan's brides?"

Everett did not take the question seriously, responding, "Then what a grand victory it will be."

As they camped for the night, Everett made a speech, "My warriors, in but a couple of days you will be part of the first great victory of my life. One day the throne shall be mine, and our kingdom and my family's crown will stretch to every corner of the earth. Statues will be built in my honour, all will bow to our flag and the scribes will pass down this story until the end of time." Everett raised his glass, "To victory."

The guards echoed, "To victory." They went to sleep that night dreaming of the glory to come.

The next day came and the rain slowed them down, as their horses feet would get stuck in the mud. Despite this setback, Everett would not be deterred. It was late into the night when they reached the village near the witch's forest. They walked into the pub and ordered their drinks and they spoke to the locals.

One man said, "I'll tell you, my sons went into that forest and I ran in after them. I heard their yelling and found them. Then I heard a voice on the wind saying 'Go, go…now!' Then a tree but 15 feet away fell over and I grabbed one son in each arm and ran like a rabbit from a dog."

Edmund once again pulled Everett aside asking if they were really enough for this mission. Everett began to insult him and question his manhood and finally stated, "You are a royal guard with an oath to fulfill. If you do any less than your duty you will be guilty of treason and put to death." Edmund immediately became silent.

That night they had their drinks to celebrate a victory for a battle that had not even started. The next day they went to the area of the forest where the folk legends had said the witch would be. Prince Everett and his guards tied up their horses on the outer trees and they went in swords raised.

The deeper they went in the slower and smaller their steps became. Finally a breeze blew by with a chilling voice saying, "Leave, now."

Prince Everett took a deep breath and said, "We are not going anywhere."

The voice came through again, "Why have you come?"

Everett loudly stated, "You owe taxes and allegiance to the crown of England. Render your payment and allegiance to me or be prepared to meet your maker."

They began to advance towards the wind that had brought her voice. As they began to walk up a hill, her voice came again, "I owe you nothing, leave me alone, or you shall be cursed."

They finished climbing the hill and saw her standing in front of her small cabin made of logs. Everett ordered his men attack when she ran inside, hid behind the door and set her locks and barricades. Edmund and Reginald began a relentless assault on the door as the others surrounded the rest of the cabin and Prince Everett looked on in anticipation.

As the door began to give way they began to hear her plead. "Leave me alone, I have no money to give you, I live off the land."

The door was barely holding when she screamed, "Leave me alone!"

Just as they broke the door down she had picked up some dust and frantically sprinkled a spice on it. Edmund and Louis charged forward when she blew the dust, which turned into fire as it left her hand and it burned Edmund and Louis, reacting they writhed on the floor. Oswald and Matthew, two of the three remaining guards grabbed her arms as Reginald grabbed her around the waist as they brought her to her knees.

Before Reginald was about to behead her, Everett stopped him and proclaimed, "Stop! This must be done by my hand." He raised his sword saying, "Your death will be glorious, your head will be our trophy."

The witch mocked, "My death will only bring the curse I have set."

Everett swung his sword and the thud of her severed skull hitting the ground echoed in her cabin as the blood sprinkled on their feet.

Reginald handed a sack to Everett as he picked the head up by its hair and put it in the sack, still dripping blood. They suddenly realized that they hadn't heard anything from Louis and Edmund and they turned around and saw them on the ground with their faces burned down to the skull.

Everett lifted the sack and proclaimed, "We are victorious, let us return to the castle with our trophy."

Reginald put his hand on Everett's shoulder saying, "It is customary for a moment of silence for the fallen."

Everett rolled his eyes, "Oh very well." They bowed their heads and their moment of silence came and went with Everett's smile growing a mile wide.

After quickly taking whatever they could they began the walk back to their horses. They began to talk about what maidens would be given to them as rewards when there was a sudden flash of blinding white light that lasted but a few seconds. Suddenly as the light faded and their eyes adjusted they were still in a forest. The trees seemed thicker and the leaves at the top were so plentiful the sun could barely shine through. Also, they now found themselves on a steeper decline. Everett and the others became nervous and Reginald asked, "I saw that light, did the witch unleash her curse?"

Trying to conceal his fear with bravado was Everett's response: "Reginald, look in this bag, this is her head, she cannot do anything. We are victorious, we will leave this forest get on our horses and ride back to the castle." Reginald let out a sigh of despair as he felt resigned to follow in Everett's hubris.

As they continued down the hill and came to the bottom of another hill, Oswald spoke up wondering if they were lost. Everett told him that the trees were getting thinner and they would be out in a few minutes. Finally they reached the top of the smaller hill but could not hear their horses but rather a different noise than they had never heard before.

They came down the hill their curiosity and confusion were obliterated by a tidal wave of shock. They saw a modern highway with cars flying by at 50 to 60 miles an hour, for the first time Everett was truly speechless. The four of them slowly approached the side of the road, the cars slowed down to stare at these shorter men in medieval clothes carrying swords. Suddenly a police car pulled over on the side of the road as two police officers came out guns drawn.

"Alright, all four of you drop your weapons!"

Prince Everett stepped forward and indignantly asked, "I am Prince Everett, who are you to give orders to me and my royal guards?"

The other officer was very slowly moving forward when he responded, "We are the West Virginia state police, if you do not drop your weapons we will have to open fire."

At the same time his partner had said into the radio, "We got some unstable people on the southbound side of the interstate, we need backup."

Everett saw two men without sword, mace or dagger who were daring to threaten him. He took two steps back and took the sack that the witch's head was in and took it out of the bag and lifted it over his head like a trophy.

He began to shake it when he proclaimed, "You will meet the same fate as this witch."

The police officer was disgusted and fearful, and with his finger on the trigger yelled, "You are all under arrest, put down your weapons and that woman's head. This is your final warning!"

Everett pointed his sword towards the officers, "Guards, attack!"

As Everett and his three remaining guards charged forward the guns fired as all four of them fell to modern might.

Two more vehicles arrived immediately after the shots to help control the situation as the shots had drawn many onlookers. Reginald looked over as he bled internally, seeing Everett writhing and screaming, "What black magic is this?"

Seeing that he was bleeding from his stomach, and that he would soon be dead, many cars had slowed to see the bizarre carnage. As Reginald looked to the road a large truck had writing on the side that declared "The best in the industry since 1993." Reading that with shock and all those people with strange clothes, talking oddly, he finally realized they weren't just somewhere else, they were in some other time. He remembered the legend of Socrates, life's moments passed like the cars that drove by and that even the Prince's bejewelled crown had been buried by the sands of time.

THE DARK CLOSET

Stephanie was scared for her friend Will, so in an act of desperation she called a professional. The professional came in and introduced herself, "Hi, I'm Dr. Melissa Li. Where is our friend today?"

Stephanie responded, "He's upstairs, he can barely get outside his bedroom. That chain is around his ankle, before he gets too far it just yanks him back in."

Dr. Melissa Li asked, "How long has he been like this?"

Stephanie responded, "As long as I've known him, so at least 3 years. Who knows how much longer?"

Melissa shook her head, "It's too bad, he's only 24, so young. How is he with talking to people?"

Stephanie said, "It varies from day to day, some days he can talk like a normal person, other days, it's like a, like a wall."

Melissa took notes as she asked if she could speak to him.

Stephanie said, "Okay, just follow me upstairs."

They walked up the stairs, as they reached the top, Stephanie pointed at the dark brown wooden door down the hall to the left and said, "That's it right there."

Melissa began to walk towards it, when Stephanie said, "Wait, let me introduce you."

Stephanie walked towards the room and knocked on the door. "Will, its Stephanie, there's someone I want you to meet, her name is Dr. Melissa Li and she wants to talk to you."

There was a pause then, Will responded by asking, "Why? I'm not sick, I feel fine."

Stephanie became tense and added, "She's a friend, please let her in."

There was a longer pause, until he said, "Okay".

Melissa slowly walked in with Stephanie, noticing the only light came in through the window next to his bed. He was sitting on the edge of his bed, attached to his right ankle was a shackle attached to a thick black chain that led to a closet across the room, under the door.

Melissa walked up to him and asked how he was doing, and also if he wanted to come downstairs. He said he was nervous, but Stephanie and Melissa told him they would help. He took a few steps towards the door and as the chain became tighter they tried to pull him towards the door when the chain yanked him back in almost no time. It dragged him across the floor when the closet door opened and closed just long enough to close behind him.

Melissa and Stephanie began to knock on the door asking him to talk to them. They could hear him begin to scream, "I can't go out there, they won't let me!" They heard him scream out in pain, as they tried to pull the closet door open, but it wouldn't budge.

Stephanie began to get really upset, "This is what always happens, why won't it get any better?"

Melissa put an arm around her and said, "It will take some time, but we will work at it."

The next week Melissa returned and sat down next to Will and asked him about the closet.

He said, "It's overwhelming, just too much."

She asked him if she could see what was inside, he said, "No, it's too painful, I don't want anyone else to deal with it."

Melissa took him by the hand, and said, "Look at your ankle, whatever is keeping you from truly going out into the world, is in that closet. Please let me help you, once it closes, it locks and only you can unlock it from the inside."

He breathed faster and heavier as the anxiety began to get to him, "I don't think I can, it's too much."

She gave him a hug, as she said, "The reason why it's overwhelming is because you are alone with it, in a small place. Please let me help you."

Before he could answer, the chain pulled again and pulled him back into the closet at lightning speed. It all happened too quickly for Melissa to get to the door before it slammed shut.

She pulled and asked for Will to open the door, but he was screaming again, "It's too late for me!" She stood there trying to encourage him but the door didn't budge.

The next week she came there and she took a different approach. She brought a rope and tied it to his arm on the opposite side. The rope was also tied to the door leading out of the room.

She then told him, "This chain is what is holding you back, this rope represents the wonderful things waiting for you out there. There is one problem, that chain is stronger than that rope, if you don't tell me how to get into that closet the rope won't help you for long."

The chain began to tighten as it pulled, but it began to pull him apart finally the rope broke and he went back in the closet again. He went back in as Melissa banged on the outside of the door, "Let me in. Let me help you, let me bring you out and help you with what's in there."

He came out a few minutes later with bruises and scratches, he said, "I don't think it's ever going to get better, thank you for trying."

Melissa went home, frustrated if only she could get in that closet, whatever was in there would be exposed.

The next week she asked him, "Don't you really want to deal with what's in that closet forever? I think if you saw what was in there you could conquer it. Right now you are fighting blind and can't find a way out."

With another anxiety filled look on his face, he asked, "What if I see it and it can't be conquered?"

She looked at him and held both of his hands in a reassuring manner, saying, "There is only one way to find out." The chain tightened and pulled him back into the closet suddenly.

Melissa banged on the door, "Come on Will, open the door, you can do it."

He was screaming in pain she said, "Open it now." She pulled as hard as she could and the door opened a crack.

She pulled harder as he said, "This has been happening since I was a child."

She pulled it open another two inches as she put a foot next to the door frame. "Keep going, don't stop now."

He continued, "It seemed like there was no escape, it was always there, waiting for me."

She pulled it open another few inches as she could see his struggle and a little bit of green skin.

He continued saying, "I have been fighting this for years…and I have had ENOUGH!"

With a loud yell he kicked the door open as hard as he could and it flung open with a bang. Melissa fell to the ground, as she looked and she saw the small green demons, there were four of them. They had small human heads but their bodies were extremely scrawny with green reptilian skin and arms and hands with claws.

He threw the second smallest one across the room, the tiny one was stomped to death as Will yelled, "You were wrong about me, I…have…a…

future." He said those last words with each stomp.

He was then struck across the face but he struck back at the second biggest one, which was about four feet tall, he proceeded to strike repeatedly at it. Melissa grabbed a lamp, as the biggest demon was about to come up behind Will as it hissed at her.

Will yelled, "I'm not you, I don't do what you say." As he bludgeoned the demon to death, the smaller one that was thrown across the room leapt at him and he grabbed it by the throat and slammed it into the ground over and over saying, "I...won't...stay...quiet, I am not your toy!"

It looked like every bone in its body was broken. Will turned around at the largest demon roughly four and a half feet tall. He charged at it and said, "I have waited for this," as he ruthlessly attacked. "You ruled my life, I was nothing but a slave to you."

With each strike, Melissa was more stunned by the intensity finally as the blood was all over the closet he let out one final scream and snapped the chain over his knee.

He leaned onto his bed exhausted, as Melissa looked at the demon corpses in his room, staring at their faces almost in disbelief.

Melissa extended her hand and said, "Let's go, it's time."

He took her hand as she helped him walk down stairs, when they walked she saw three of the demon's faces on the family portraits on the wall. As they came downstairs, they walked through the living room. She saw the smallest demon's face in his fourth grade class picture on the mantle.

It had been so long since he had seen more than what little sunlight would shine through the window. He came closer and closer to the door, Melissa stopped turned him around and said "As great as things can be out there, there are a lot of other demons and a lot of other chains, please watch out for them."

He gave Melissa a big hug as he turned the knob for the door and he opened it wide and stepped through that door, into the bright enveloping sunlight. Just before he closed the door behind him he took one look back and said, "No more chains, no more demons, just me." That door closing behind him not only felt empowering it was the sweetest sound he had ever heard.

LEAVE IT ALL BEHIND

It was a beautiful day in June, somewhere not too far from the Caribbean a private cruise was travelling with about 40 passengers. A hole was made in the boat by a loose but sharp stick. The captain announced the issue and that while they were repairing the ship they would be pulled up on a small uncharted island. Derek and Hillary, a couple on their vacation, were the only ones not bothered by the delay. They were on vacation, "Anything is better than work," ran through both their minds.

As the ship pulled up on the shore the captain and three other cruise employees made the following announcement: "Feel free to look around, this Island is roughly a mile and a half across, but be back here in three hours so we can get back on track."

Derek whispered in Hillary's ear, "Let's get wild in the forest."

Hillary nodded with a mischievous smile, as they drifted into the forest. They found a spot somewhat deep in the forest and they began having sex as their passions overcame them. The taboo of being outside, of being in such primal surroundings this new exciting situation added an entirely new level of spark to what had previously been a sex life stuck in neutral.

As they were putting on their clothes, both relieved and enthralled by their experience, they heard a loud scream some distance away. Fearing that someone was hurt, Derek and Hillary ran towards the direction of the scream. As they grew closer they could hear the yelling.

"You distracted me!"

"You should have watched where you were going, asshole."

Derek became concerned, wondering what sort of fight was about to break out.

A couple other people showed up and someone asked, "Hey what's happening?"

One of the guys said, "I nearly fell down this hole."

Derek asked, "How deep is it?"

No one answered, so to fulfill his curiosity Derek picked up a small rock and dropped it in the hole. A few seconds went by and they heard nothing.

"Okay, that would have been bad, good thing you didn't fall in," Hillary said.

One of the two men who had been arguing spoke up, "Maybe we should all get back to the ship, who knows what other traps like this are lying around."

They all looked at each other, Derek and Hillary looked around, seeing a wooden ladder leading down several feet.

"You weren't kidding about this being a trap," another one chimed in.

"What do you think is down there?" Derek asked.

One of the two men who appeared responded, "I don't know but I have a bad feeling about this." They all began to walk back towards the shore Derek and Hillary began to lag behind the others as Derek looked at that hole in the ground with a warped curiosity.

He whispered in her ear, "I'm not like these other guys, I'm not afraid to see what's down there."

Hillary said with a little bit of caution, "Are you sure?"

He looked back at her, "Hillary, I spend an hour a day sitting in a car driving too and from work, I spend 40 hours a week sitting in an office looking at a computer screen, I am bored as hell and I didn't spend almost $2,000 just to sit on a beach. I want to be able to say I did something daring."

She looked slightly offended, "Having sex with me in the middle of a forest, in the middle of an uncharted island wasn't daring?"

Derek responded with a cocky swagger, "I was just getting started, I'm going down there."

He walked back towards the hole, as Hillary grabbed his arm, "Look, I am all for having an adventure, but I don't like this."

He kissed her, "I got this."

He took a few steps down the ladder, and the top of the hole was up to his shoulders.

Hillary handed him her cell phone, "Use this to light your way, you should at least be able to see where you are going."

He rolled his eyes, "Okay, but I told you I have got this." As he took more and more steps down he fell out of the sunlight and just as he was barely even visible.

Hillary called out to him, "What's happening down there?"

Derek called back up, "Everything is fine, I think I'm near the bottom."

When he felt a hand try to grab at his ankle he turned the cell phone and saw a deformed woman's face scowling at him, as her eyes nearly glowed with rage.

He yelled out, "Holy shit!" as he raced back up the ladder as quickly as he could.

He made it up to the top of the ladder he grabbed Hillary by the hand, "We need to go now!"

With great urgency they raced away and they heard something from the hole screaming. Hillary briefly stopped and turned around, asking, "What the hell is going on?"

Derek kept pulling, "We need to leave now."

As they raced into the trees in the same direction as the others Derek's heart pounded, wondering what sort of hideous creature he had awoken. As they raced to the shore they saw a few of the other people talking to the captain.

They raced towards the captain as they heard the captain saying, "You found a what ship?"

The other couple said, "A slave ship, it had shackles and everything."

Derek suddenly interrupted, "We found something too, something was down the hole, a person or something."

The captain paused and called out, "Everyone, please come here! Okay, it turns out the ship's damage is worse than expected, so we are going to be here until tomorrow morning. For everyone's safety please stay here along the shore-line and don't go anywhere alone. Whether other people are here on the island or not, we should avoid splitting up, I don't want anyone to accidentally get left behind. Are we clear?"

Everyone nodded as Derek took a look at his ankle to make sure it wasn't hurt, seeing there were no marks as he was relieved.

Hillary went to talk to the other couple who had been talking to the captain, "Tell me about this ship?"

The man began to talk, "We found it a little bit into the island up that way."

Hillary continued, "What was in there?"

The woman took over, "It was stunning! It was pretty big, it looked like it was over 100 years old. We came back because we wanted some people to go with us, would you and your husband like to come with us?"

Her eyes lit up, "Sure, find a few other people and we'll go."

Derek felt a cold chill run down his spine as he saw the sun was setting too, knowing in an hour it would be dark.

Hillary found Derek and told him that they were going to the other ship wreckage, he took a deep breath and said, "Okay, I just hope there aren't any others out there."

The other couple came up to them with two other men saying, "I think we should be safe if there are six of us."

The captain came up to them asking, "Where do you think you are going?"

Hillary responded, "We are going to see the ship they saw."

The Captain said, "Six of you will probably be okay, but if you see any issues come back before dark. We are leaving at 11 am and I don't want to have to go looking for anybody."

They started to walk along the shore towards the ship wreckage as Hillary said, "This is so exciting."

Derek was struggling to put that moment from a mere 40 minutes ago behind him. He held Hillary's hand tighter, she looked at him recognizing his fear.

"Was it really that horrible, was that person really so ugly?"

He responded, "It wasn't just ugly, it was deformed. The jaw was like, protruding out and the nose was misshapen and those eyes were expressionless. That mouth was angry like an animal whose territory I crossed into."

A small chill ran down her spine as well as she saw the fear in his face, "It was dark, it might not have been that bad."

As she said it, she knew he saw something horrible but she stepped forward hoping that maybe this ship would give them the clue about the mysterious warped person.

They approached the ship that was several yards onto the shore with old worn ropes around it, leaning on its right side as if it had been dragged onto the shore. Parts of the ship had collapsed on itself as if it had slowly fallen apart and had been there for a few centuries, worn down and weathered by years of storms. As they approached the back of the ship the sun became completely out of view as the bright blue sky began to grow darker. The couple pointed to the hole that was roughly two feet across and eighteen inches wide, large enough for them to see what was inside.

The woman who had found the ship with her husband mentioned that if the men worked at it they could rip the remaining wood panels off the bottom of the ship. The men did exactly that while Hillary and the other woman watched.

The other woman asked Hillary, "Do you really think there are people underground somehow? I mean where did they come from, if they are from this ship, that's at least 200 years old, how did they survive all this time?"

Hillary responded, "I don't know, but it will be nice solving a mystery as opposed to getting some polite version of the 'You don't need to know' answer I get way too often at the office."

After much pulling and grunting they ripped off several boards leaving a tear large enough for any of them to step into. They stepped into the bottom of the ship they saw the shackles as well as a few skeletons that had barely held together. They wondered what had happened as several of the shackles had clearly been opened.

As they went deeper into the ship, Hillary began to sneeze at the remarkable amount of dust that had built up in that time. They walked towards the partially broken stairs that were now sideways, they were chilled to see spots of near black, dried blood that were on the stairs and the rail. They decided that trying to climb up would be dangerous so they decided to go around to the top of the ship.

They went up to the top of the ship where they climbed a nearby tree to get onto the ship, the angle making the climb difficult, Derek led the climb as he was having a second wind of courage and there had been no sign of the deformed people. He pulled himself up as his curiosity drew him to the captain's quarters. He got closer and closer as he reached for the doorknob, however, as he pulled, it came off and he fell backward into one of the other men. He pulled himself back up and he kicked the door in as it flew open and the stench of century's old dust made him cough. He looked around he opened the desk and saw an old log of aged, yellow paper. He picked it up wondering, imagining what led to this.

He got back with the other two men who had come up, and Derek began reading through the log. He flipped to the final page and the last entry read as follows: "October 18, 1603: We are close to the end of the journey, we just landed on this undiscovered island this morning, hopefully we can repair the ship and finish the journey to South Carolina."

Derek showed this to Hillary as they saw something in the distance through the trees. Hillary and Derek began to walk towards it, as they got closer they saw some half collapsed huts.

They were drawn in, they couldn't stop themselves from wondering what had occurred, and as they stepped inside they noticed the chains attached to the makeshift bed.

Derek looked at Hillary, "My god, what kind of sick people came off this ship."

Hillary looked back at him, "Slave owners."

They looked through a few of the other huts and saw something similar on one of the huts was a dark red bloodstain on the wall. As they came out they knew they were numerous yards into the forest, the blue sky had almost turned black and they began to hear some noises around them.

"Derek, I think we need to get out of here, it might be them."

Derek ripped two of the loose sticks from the wall of the nearest hut and handed one to Hillary, "If we back out slowly and keep these in hand we should be fine."

Derek and Hillary gradually walked back towards the ship and they heard the voice of one of their fellow searchers, "Derek, Hillary, where are you!"

Suddenly from behind one of the huts they heard a piercing shriek, a war cry that sent chills through Derek and Hillary's whole skeletons. They immediately ran back towards the cruise ship, yelling along the way, "They're here! There's a lot of them, run!"

They all ran away from the ship, towards the shoreline and one of the others was grabbed and dragged back into the forest. Hillary and Derek were running as hard as they could in complete fear for their lives, by the time they got back to the shore where the others were, they had reached complete panic.

The captain asked, "Where are the others?"

Derek blurted out, "They took them, those deformed people."

The captain began yelling, "What, are you kidding me? That's it! This has gone too far, we need to call the police and get them out here."

Hillary spoke up, "That will be too late, they might kill them, and if we have to wait until morning, who knows how much longer until they come after the rest of us. We're the only ones that can save them."

Derek's eyes nearly popped out of his head. "What, we aren't the Avengers, we don't even know what we are dealing with."

She responded, "Look, you woke these things up, we know where they are and we're going to save these people."

The captain turned away looking out into the ocean. He let out a big sigh as he turned to everyone looking back at him.

"Our number one priority is getting off this island alive. I cannot in good conscience lead a war against some unknown enemy. How many of them are there 20? 30? 100? I have no idea, but there is no way I am leading the people whose lives I am entrusted with into something dangerous. I was too reckless letting you into the forest in the first place. That ship where this incident happened, is it still intact?"

The couple that originally discovered it spoke up, "For the most part, the wood is old and some of it is dilapidated."

The captain said with a lamenting look on his face, "It's the only option we have, we don't have time to cut down trees and carve them, especially with this threat. Maybe we can harvest that ship for parts and get out of here before it gets too late."

Hillary spoke up, "Well you can do that, but Derek, myself and anyone else that has the guts is going to save them."

Everyone else looked at each other to contemplate their next move, as several of them began to walk towards the captain about 15 of them, a few more went towards the captain a moment later. Finally about 11 of them walked towards Hillary and Derek, as the lines were drawn.

The captain said to them, "If you go with them, I take no responsibility for what happens to you."

Julian spoke up, "That's fine, but if we are all going to get home we have to get the two of us that are missing." It was becoming the dark of night, the blue sky was clouding over turning black. They each had their role; Derek and Hillary pulled their people aside.

Derek began, "Thank you all, just to warn you we are dealing with some dangerous deformed people, they were almost acting like animals. Whatever the case with these people are, it could get really ugly, but if we don't do something, I don't want to think about what could happen to them."

Hillary spoke up, "Now is not the time for speeches, we have to get going. The hole is this way."

As they all began walking one of them spoke up, "I think we need some light, I have two lighters, let's make some torches."

Hillary spoke up, "Let's not draw them too us, let's get those ready just before we go in."

As they continued walking Hillary whispered to Derek, "What do you think we will find down there?"

He responded, "I don't know, hopefully just a few of them, and they will give back the others without a fight when they see our numbers."

Hillary whispered, "Do you really think it will be that easy?"

He responded, "I don't know anymore."

They walked closer and closer as the dread filled everyone, finally one of them burst out, "This is crazy, screw this!" and went running away.

Everyone looked at each other wondering if anyone else was thinking the same thing. After a brief awkward pause Derek spoke up, "Everyone, the hole is just a few more steps away, people's lives are at stake, if you want out this is your last chance."

There was another pause and then Hillary said, "Okay, we're going in."

Those last few steps led them all right to the edge of the hole and Derek took a deep breath. He pulled out his cell phone to light the area as he climbed down, and another person began to climb down after him. The memories of what had already happened began to make him sweat, his hands were clammy just as his feet touched the ground his left foot was right next to the stone that had been dropped earlier as he knocked it to the side.

He turned around flashing the light in all directions looking for things, as he began to walk in the others began to land on the ground. He flashed his light around, he began to walk to the corner that turned right, as he approached the bend, his foot hit something hard and he looked down and saw a small skull on the ground. He took a step back as two others joined him to look at it.

One of the guys who came over said to him, "This is some bad shit, I'm expecting Freddy Krueger or Jason Voorhees or some other thing to pop out."

Derek's fear was becoming more transparent, as Hillary came over, "Look honey, you can do this, I believe in you." She grabbed both his cheeks with both hands and kissed him, "We can do this."

Julian had walked around the corner, where there was another turn to the left. He looked back as the others followed, but he began walking back.

"What's wrong?" Derek asked.

"Not enough light, I'm going to rip off a couple branches from the trees and make some torches."

As Julian climbed back up the ladder, they waited there moving their cell phones around just to keep aware when Hillary flashed her light around the corner of the second turn to see one of the deformed men staring at them. There was a piercing scream then he went back, yelling in some almost ani- malistic call. The man who suggested the torches came back down the ladder with half a dozen branches and took his shirt off and began ripping it to wrap around the to make torches. They waited there with their lights flashed to the corner awaiting an attack from more of the deformed, as the torches began to be lit.

Derek took one saying, "Thanks..." and Julian responded, "Julian." They went around the second corner preparing for the worst, but their preparations were not enough for what they were going to see.

They turned the corner and saw an altar where there was a small child's dead body being chewed by two of the deformed people. They saw old barrels of liquor as well as numerous sets of shackles where their friends were. They heard that same animalistic yell from the deformed man pointing at them as they saw several of these deformed people emerge. Some of them moved slowly as if their limbs had grown improperly and others were missing teeth and several had scars on them as if this horrible place had to perpetuate its own ugliness.

One of the captured said, "There are a few dozen of them, get out of here now."

Julian spoke up, "Do any of you speak English?"

There was a tense pause followed by a stomping foot as two of them charged, forcing Derek and another man to use their torches to hold them off. As the few dozen slowly approached, Hillary and another woman, Anita, were ripping the shackles off the wall, having seen that they were loose.

Derek quietly asked Julian as they moved their torches back and forth, "What are we going to do?"

Julian looked over at the barrels of alcohol and said, "We may have to light this sucker on fire."

As the deformed people got closer and closer, Derek looked in their faces hoping for something human, instead finding the intense attack mode of wild animals. As Hillary and another woman finished getting both of the captives free, Julian swung the torch forcing a few of them back as he ran to the barrels and began to throw them as the barrels hit some of them and smashed on the ground. All of them began to go towards Julian, as the others ran for the tunnel. Right after he threw the fourth barrel, they got him and began to scratch and claw at him.

Derek and Hillary looked at each other and swung the torches to force them back. Derek threw two more barrels back towards the entrance, the torches keeping them angry and at bay. Julian pulled himself back up behind Derek and Hillary as they began to inch backwards, past the barrel that had only partially broken and still had close to half of its original contents. They began to resume their attack formation, knowing everyone else was either going or gone. In one last act, Julian lowered his torch to set the barrel on fire and throw it at them. The screams were chilling, as they ran all the smashed liquor caused the fire to spread quickly. They ran as fast as they could back up the ladder and Derek lit the top of the ladder on fire and they ran for the shore.

They all finally got to the shore where they all struggled to catch their breaths, Julian was bleeding from where he was scratched and clawed. The person who had left before they entered the hole ran up to them, "Holy shit, what happened?"

Hillary spoke up, "We got everyone out alive, that's… that's what matters."

Derek chimed in, "What about the ship? Can they fix it?"

The other man responded, "Yes, in fact he said we can leave in a few hours."

He walked on to tell the others the news, Julian shook his head in disbelief, "This wasn't in the brochure."

They each let out an uncomfortable chuckle, "In all seriousness, I thought I was done for. You saved my ass and I'll never forget that as long as I live."

Hillary said, "You're welcome, but I would go to a doctor; you don't want those to get infected and who knows what diseases those people had." He shook their hands and left.

Everyone waited on the shore, there was still a clear division, between who stayed and who left for the hole. All who had been inside were staring at the forest fearing the deformed people's arrival while the others continued working on the ship or talking amongst themselves as if they were still on vacation.

The tension continued to creep in as they waited until finally the captain declared, "Get your things and get on this ship."

People scurried on as quickly as they could everyone wanted to get as far away from this nightmarish place as soon as possible. As the ship was a moment away from leaving the island, Derek and Hillary walked to the front deck to keep a look out as they would finally leave.

"Derek, how does a place get like this?"

Derek paused before responding, "Well, I guess when terrible people land in an isolated place and use shackles to keep everyone trapped, all you have is… barbarism."

She responded, "The irony is that those slave owners thought they were the civilized ones."

Derek responded, "Yeah, but even with all that, I still have the captain's journal, if the captain of that old ship was in charge I think he would have kept it with him."

She looked at him for a moment and then back to the island, "So you think it was mutiny?"

Derek shrugged saying, "Maybe."

Hillary continued in a disturbed tone, "Followed by rape, slavery, and incest with no escape? My God, those poor people."

The ship began to move

"We're on our way!" The captain declared, with enthusiasm and relief.

Derek let out a sigh, "I guess that is what happened, we'll never know for sure. But as horrible as it is, at least we get to leave, and with all that fire they are probably gone." As they began to walk towards the rest of the people on the ship they heard one of those skeleton-chilling shrieks from the island. They both looked back at that horrible place that the ship was leaving when Hillary, in horrified disbelief asked, "It's still not over, when it will be?"

THE EYES OF GOD

A very long time ago, in a forgotten era, in a place that's been renamed repeatedly, were two young girls, Marita and Cordella. Marita and Cordella were as close as sisters but were friends, Cordella was just a few months older. Cordella and Marita looked up at the sky, not with wonder but with despair. They were tired of seeing the eyes of God watching them. One came out to light up the day, the other lit up the night.

As Cordella's 13th birthday grew closer, she knew that she was going to be forced to be one of the elder's wives. She had seen how the elders treated their current wives and dreaded each passing day. With her 13th birthday just two months away she asked her mother, "Why must I marry the elder?"

Her mother said with outrage, "How dare you question the law! The elders must have five wives; if one dies another who has just turned 13 must take her place. It is a privilege that you should be grateful for."

By this point Cordella had been told that anything she did wrong would be seen by the eyes and told to the elders, and that harsh punishments would follow. The thought of being groped by that arrogant old man made her skin crawl and her stomach warp.

One night after her chores, Marita came over to Cordella's house where Cordella took her into a quiet corner of the house. While her family was distracted by other visitors, Cordella said in a paranoid and quiet voice, "We need to get out of here, I can't marry the elder."

Marita's jaw dropped, she looked around and whispered, "Are you crazy? We couldn't leave even if we tried. We'd get 20 feet away from the village and God would tell the elders and we would get dragged back and beaten."

Cordella took a deep breath, "I don't care, I can't live like this. I'd rather die, and if I leave you might be next and you would be miserable forever."

The reality of the situation swept across Marita and she felt the same dread as Cordella, but didn't know what she was about to suggest.

"So what do you want to do?"

Cordella looked around again, "I can only think of one way; maybe if there are enough clouds, God's eyes will be covered, and if it is dark enough that people can't see, it's our only chance, we have to do it soon."

Marita's eyes lit up, "What do you mean soon? Your marriage isn't for two more months."

Cordella responded saying, "The closer we get to my 13th birthday, the closer they will watch me."

Marita was still scared of the idea, "What about our families?"

Cordella let out a sigh, "I will miss my family too, but this is our only chance and our families would only try to stop us."

Marita asked, "What will we do?"

Cordella responded, "Figure out what you need to take, and on a night with heavy clouds, we will leave."

As Cordella said goodbye to Marita, they looked up and saw the night sky filled with stars and only a few clouds to the west. They looked at each other with a look of "not tonight." The next two nights went by, as the sky filled with more clouds, but not enough to cover God's eyes for more than a few minutes. However, it was enough to give Cordella hope. The next day she saw one of the elder's wives and she came up to Cordella, saying her, "Soon you will be joining us, just remember that I outrank you and if the elder isn't around you will do what I say."

The elder's wife walked away causing Cordella to become filled with dread again. They were beginning to watch, she knew her time was running out.

She looked up at the sky as it was filling up with clouds, seeing God's brighter eye only partially covered. She had everything that she was taking with her figured out and had to hope that when the time came no one would stop her. She also had to hope that Marita would be willing to go all the way with the journey, Cordella and Marita knew only too well what they had to sacrifice.

Cordella woke up the next morning, knowing that this was the day she would leave her family forever. She looked at her younger brother and sister as she began to tear up, knowing she couldn't say goodbye. As she looked up and saw God's fiery eye barely peaking through, she knew she might have only one chance.

That night the sky became a darker blue with grey clouds, Cordella came up with a lie to tell her parents why she would be gone for hours. She came to Marita and they were about to leave, Marita said, "If we leave, we better put as much distance between us and the village as possible. If we get caught we will be beaten and scarred. A woman named Dara tried to escape six years ago and that's why she still has those scars on her arms and back."

Cordella took a deep breath, "Well, we must go now."

It was dark, but their eyes adjusted as they got away from town. Marita was moving quickly with the new fear of the beating fresh in her mind. With each step they took they knew they would have to make two more to keep themselves away from the village. They walked for hours, every few minutes looking behind them for the hunters that they were sure would be after them. They talked quietly and they picked up what they could along the way, Cordella picked up a rock that was almost too big for her to hold with a slightly dull point.

"What do we need that for?" Marita asked.

Cordella responded, "In case we need food, or we need to fight back."

Hours went by, their feet ached, and the small amount of food and water they had brought was almost done. Their eyes became heavy and the sky began to lighten up. They saw a forest some distance away, and knew that they had to fall asleep without being exposed. They ran and ran, looking above for fear of one of the eyes of God seeing them. Before the sunrise came over the horizon they had put themselves 200 metres deep into the forest and found a comfortable place to lie down. That morning they went to sleep, Cordella and Marita did so knowing that when they woke up they would wake up to a different world and a different life.

Six hours later, the birds chirped as Cordella woke up, and she looked around. She became scared realizing that they were trapped, God's eye was shining through some of the leaves. If God's eye didn't see them before, it would see them for sure if they left the forest now. They looked around for food and to watch out for places where they might be seen directly.

Cordella and Marita held hands as Cordella said, "We have to stick together, no matter what happens."

The next day, there was some rain in the morning as they were considering how they would survive. Cordella said, "We can wait a little while, but we can't stay here forever. The next time the clouds completely block out either of the eyes of God we have to keep going."

Marita responded, "We can't leave, we were lucky to find this forest, where else can hide us from the eyes of God?"

Cordella said, "Maybe another village has elders that will defend us?"

Marita said, "Are you crazy? Our only hope is to stay here."

Cordella and Marita began to argue and shout over each other. Marita finally said, "I am not leaving this forest and you can't make me!"

Cordella stomped away in frustration, as she wanted to look and see what she could see beyond the forest. She walked to the edge of the forest where she saw no sign of anyone, but saw what looked like a river in the distance. She looked and realized that if she followed the river they could find another society. She wanted to go back and try to talk to Marita about what she had found. She followed the path back to where she and Marita had been, as she got closer she heard a scream in the distance and she ran as quickly as she could, she ran faster when she heard more screaming and she knew it was Marita's voice. As she came over the last hill, she saw Marita being forced down by a man, her clothes having been ripped off.

Cordella still had the rock she had left with and she picked it up as she charged at the attacker. With one hard strike he was knocked over, holding his head as Cordella hit him again and again, each strike more furious than the one before. Marita finally declared while covering herself, "He's dead! He's dead!!"

The blood that poured out of his head began to pool on the ground and had stained half of the rock Cordella was holding, and her fingertips. As Cordella looked back at Marita they embraced, relieved that the other was okay and that they still had each other. Cordella looked at her, "See, we can't stay here, we have to go." They packed their belongings and walked towards the edge of the forest where Cordella had seen the river.

Cordella's hand was sore from the impact of the strikes and was trying to massage the inside of her hand so it would feel better. As they approached the edge of the forest, Marita began to retreat.

"No way, the eye will see us."

Cordella had not come this far to stop now. She turned to Marita, "I can't stay hiding in a forest and I'm not going to hide for the rest of my life. I have to go out there." Marita put her hand over her mouth frightened to death of what was about to happen.

Cordella took one bold step after another until she was clearly in the light and she faced it defiantly.

"God, we're not going back, if you are against us, then throw a bolt of lightning and strike me dead."

Marita watched and cringed, waiting for the wrath, the wrath that she had been told her whole life was sure to come, but there was silence.

Cordella proclaimed even louder. "God don't send the elders after us, if you are so powerful, stop us yourself. If you don't wish for us to go somewhere else then strike me down, crush me like an ant, I await your wrath."

Minutes went by but there was no wrath, just a cool breeze, as Cordella looked back at Marita, "God isn't going to stop us, there is a river over there, let's go and see where it leads."

Marita nervously stepped into the sunlight, "What if God has just told the elders where we are?"

Cordella responded, "God isn't going to stop us but our village's enforcers will, which is why we have to get even further away from our village."

They walked into the distance as they approached the bend in the river, they saw which way the river was flowing and followed it. Marita continued to look in the sky for fear of the eye, wondering if God's wrath awaited or if the elder's enforcers were on their way. As night fell, they had not eaten since that morning and their exhaustion and hunger were beginning to overwhelm them when they saw a village very different from their own.

When they finally walked in, someone came to them speaking a different dialect of their language. The people of this village fed them and welcomed them with open arms. When the chief asked them where they came from, Cordella and Marita told their story. The chief nodded his head as they spoke, his face increasingly displaying disbelief, disappointment, and sympathy. Once Cordella had finished her story, the chief spoke, "Your elders lied to you, those are not eyes. One is a torch created so we can see the world during the day, and the other that appears at night is like ice on the lake, the cold disk shines the light of the angel's candles. All of those small lights that we see at night, like the candles we light when we lose one of our own."

Cordella looked at Marita in confusion, this seemed so odd because the chief spoke with such certainty. The chief went on, "If you wish to stay with us you may. We do not force anyone to be married. Man or woman, your voice shall be heard. If you were not meant to be heard you would never have been given the ability to speak, that is why the animals remain quiet or say nothing."

Marita's face showed a renewed excitement and relief, "What if the enforcers of our village come, will you protect us?"

The chief responded, "Yes, once you join us, we protect you as we protect our own family. Are you ready to become one of us?"

Marita jumped in whole heartedly, "I will be happy to join, what must I do?"

The chief said, "You must proclaim your heart to our village and to our creator."

Cordella was unsure, but as she looked around, realizing what few options she had, she took a deep breath and agreed. Every day after that, Cordella looked over her shoulder for fear of the enforcers from her village coming to drag them back. She wondered if this village's men could fight them off or if they would be overwhelmed. Every day she tried to tell herself it was over and she was safe, but the fear persisted, the occasional nightmare that she had didn't help this fear. A few weeks later she decided to step away from the village and looked at the ball of ice in the sky. She looked at it and couldn't tell what it was, it was closer and bigger than it had been in a long time. She began to think that maybe the elders of her village and the chief of this one were both wrong, and how she couldn't believe either.

However she looked back at this new village that welcomed her with open arms. She thought, "Maybe I can question. After all I have a voice, and in this village they value what I have to say." She looked back at that large white something in the night sky and for the first time, the eye of God was blind and her life was hers. As for whether her questions would be answered she felt strong enough to speak up and be heard, although she had no idea whether anyone would listen.

YEAR ZERO

On June 6, 2209, a group of scientists across multiple disciplines held a large press conference to announce that Project Limitless was no longer hypothetical, no longer a dream, it was not only possible but feasible.

Dr. Patel took the stage, "As most of you know, our sun is the source of light, heat, vitamin D and unfortunately sunburns." He paused for the mild laughter, "However our sun is also an enormous ticking time bomb which, in a few billion years, will change into a red star and make our planet so hot it would be unable to sustain life for humans or any other species that we are aware of. While past projects did attempt to reverse the sun's aging process we discovered that we would have to bankrupt the planet just to reverse the sun's age by 700-800 years.

"There had to be a better way, and we found one with our new series of gravitational engines that work off of a combination of gravitational energy and solar power. These engines will be able to propel the earth in any direction, in order to sustain them and ourselves we will also have our own miniature sun that will orbit the earth and allow us to retain the climate conditions that we are used to. With this incredible combination, we will in time be able to go to any solar system we wish, we will be able to avoid any possible asteroids. Best of all, with this investment we are one big step closer to guaranteeing the survival of an immortal human dynasty."

One reporter asked, "When can it be done?"

Dr. Patel responded, "Once the money and organization comes together we estimate it will take 8-10 years for construction and implementation."

By 2227, Project Limitless had a large degree of public support and was getting ready to begin. The 23rd century was becoming defined for its optimism about the future, believing the conflict-ridden 20th and 21st centuries were left far behind in their rear view mirror.

One big threat to the project remained, in the 22nd a century a few terrorist groups had come together against the notion of "the immortal human dynasty." While several of them had fallen away, by the 2170's the remaining two groups had united and had made their mission to ensure humanity went extinct as they claimed it "had to."

Marcus, along with his security team, was called into the meeting they had waited for. The commander spoke to them with the most serious tone he ever had.

"January 1, 2228 will also be known as January 1, Year Zero. This will be a new beginning for us all, we are dealing with forces of energy so great that we must protect it. As you know that terrorist group 'The Natural Way' wants this launch to fail and there is no telling what they may try. You are the last line of defence, if somehow they get in this facility, you must stop them at any cost. I mean it, at any cost, even your own lives. That will be all."

Marcus took a look at the calendar seeing November 26, 2227, it seemed so odd flipping the calendar screen forward for it to say January 0000.

Allison sat down next to him, "As horrible as this sounds, a part of me hopes The Natural Way tries something so we can take some of them out."

Marcus rolled his eyes, "Allison, you are a great soldier, but you are forgetful."

Allison looked at him, "I didn't forget three years ago when they kidnapped and killed two people who worked at the South Africa site and we had to modify all of our procedures to make sure they couldn't hack in."

Marcus looked at her shaking his head, "How many of the people who died in the 20th and 21st centuries had that attitude?"

Allison rolled her eyes and in a slightly sarcastic voice repeated what she had been told her whole life, "I know, all over the world in every country are fields of grass genetically engineered blood red to remind everyone of the bloodshed of the wars and revolutions that haunt our history."

Marcus looked at her, "So you do you remember, you are just ignoring it."

Fazil interjected, "Hey everyone, we aren't here for a philosophy debate, Marcus, you can't hesitate if they come, because they won't. Allison, don't be too eager, if they get in this room, we are all in trouble; we are the last line of defence."

December went on as they ran drill after drill, Marcus repeated to himself all the procedures and the warning signs. As each day passed everyone was excited for the beginning of a new era, there were interviews on the Internet with couples who had their baby in incubation who were due in January.

The stories were upbeat as the news anchor spoke, "In these incubators are the babies of a new era, the new golden age of humankind, a recent poll suggests that 76% are extremely optimistic about the future, 12% are somewhat optimistic 9% are undecided and 3% are pessimistic. What this shows is the progress we are making and the hope for the future generations."

On December 28th, the Government of the United Planet had received a threat from The Natural Way, using masks and voice distorters. The video was shown to the government personnel such as the soldiers:

"Humanity is a virus, they have destroyed species, and they have made a mockery of natural selection and nature. You will finally fall as all must fall, you have polluted the world and made it filthy and impure. Your arrogant desire for an immortal dynasty will end and mankind's judgment day is very near."

In order to avoid various problems, this video was not released to the public.

The next day the security team had a meeting, the commander said, "As suspected, The Natural Way is planning something, judging from their rhetoric they may be planning to use the engines or the artificial sun to kill billions of people and billions of other species. We are on maximum alert, I expect all of you to be at your best."

During the last few days security was so tight that the normal 30 seconds for each person to enter was turned into two minutes. The tension grew and grew, so much so that the day of December 31st the team spoke of the nightmares they had the night before. With just 8 hours before the launch everyone braced themselves for what they feared would come.

Kenta reminded Marcus of the prevented chemical weapon plot of 2196, that would have killed tens of millions had it succeeded, and how panic would have reigned if the public knew about it. With all of this racing through his mind, celebrating New Year's was nowhere on his radar.

The launch was a mere 20 minutes away when the first explosion went off. The gates were breached as the alarm sounded and the commander exclaimed, "This is it, they're coming in! But they are leaving in cuffs or body bags."

The grenades went off as The Natural Way's hijacked helicopter crashed into one of the walls. Allison loaded her weapon, Marcus and Kenta loaded theirs as they looked and saw the launch was 16 minutes away.

Rizalyn was listening on the radio, "Six other engine bases are being attacked, and none have breached any cores."

Marcus began to open fire as he tried to pick them off in the sweeping motion he had practiced so many times. As he looked deeper, he saw that this was an army of several thousand on its way, he knew that they could not hold them off for too long. The reinforcements needed were still some distance away, an attack of this scale had not even been imagined.

Despite everything he had been trained to do, he left his post and approached the commander. "We have to shut down the engines, if they get control of even one engine they can push our planet in a fatal direction."

The commander responded, "Get back to your post soldier."

Marcus stood his ground, "Commander, unless the reinforcements arrive the next three to five minutes we have to shut them down and get the other locations to do likewise if they are about to be breached."

The commander took another look through the lens of his rifle seeing the thousands coming at them, "Damn it your right. We'll get Rizalyn to give that order and you will accompany Jason to the engines hard drives. Let's go soldier. Everyone else keep firing!"

The commander and Marcus went straight to Rizalyn for status updates, "Engines 1 and 2 are secure, 3 is under heavy fire, 4, 6 and 7 are secure, ours and 8 are losing barriers quickly. 9 and 10 are secure, 11 has captured the insurgents and 12 is still a hot zone." Suddenly another explosion rang out as Rizalyn's screen flashed red, "Tunnel B has been breached, they're coming!"

The commander turned to Marcus with great urgency, "Take Justin to the engine, the only way they are taking it is over our dead bodies."

Marcus and Justin rushed down the ladders to the engine. As they ran they heard a shake of the tunnels above, they kept going. Finally Justin the technician entered his clearance and began the shutdown procedure.

"In 5 minutes, this engine will fully shut down and it will take 11 hours to reboot it, which should be enough time."

Marcus heard someone coming as the echo was bounced off the metal walls he looked at the timer saying 04:55 and feared they didn't even have that. As he poked his head around the corner he saw Allison coming and he said, "What's happening up there?"

She responded, "The reinforcements will get here soon, but the commander is dead. They are coming!"

They both stood behind the wall of sub-tunnel C awaiting the invaders arrival. "What's the plan?" Allison asked.

Marcus responded, "We are shutting the engines down, we just need to hold them for four more minutes."

The first Natural Way Soldier's feet touched the ground as Marcus and Allison aimed and waited for the second one to touch. With their pulses racing they opened fire as one of the Natural Way was killed, but the others began to fire back. Each second was an eternity; finally one shot hit Allison in the stomach and struck Marcus in the shoulder as they both fell stunned.

Five men came over as their leader said, "Hold these two, we might need one of them." Their leader and two of their soldiers went to where the engine's hard drive was. Marcus knew he had seconds before they would find Justin and realize they were unnecessary.

He began to speak quietly as if he couldn't speak, as the soldier guarding him came close to hear what he was saying, he grabbed the bottom of the other soldier's gun, pulled him down and wrapped his legs around the other soldiers head and snapped his neck in one fluid motion. Before the other soldier could react Allison dislocated his knee with a single kick and snapped his neck in similar fashion.

Allison asked him, "Can you move?"

Marcus nodded, and she responded, "Then go and finish this I will stay here and fire if anyone else comes down."

Marcus saw her lying on the ground fearing the worst, "Are you sure? You may not have long."

She responded, "I can't get up, but I can put my finger on the trigger, that is all we need, now go!"

Marcus struggled to run knowing he might already be too late, as he forced himself towards the engine. As he approached he heard, "Stop stalling and turn off that timer, it says 45 seconds, stop it now."

Marcus came in the room just as they shot Justin, and he attacked one of their soldiers as the other one jumped on him. He struggled to free his arms as their leader began to press the screen. Marcus was beginning to get wrestled to the ground as he elbowed one of the soldiers in the face and punched the other in the throat. He shot one as he grabbed the leader from around his waist and threw him to the ground.

Marcus began, "You are under arrest for attempted genocide and mass murder. You're going away for a long time."

Their leader began to laugh, "In a few hours, the laws of man will be meaningless, their pre-destined extinction becomes reality at last. The time of the prophecy has come and we will all see it happen."

Marcus saw that the engine had been activated and knew that the earth was being moved and knew that the earth was being pushed towards the sun. With no idea what to do he shot their leader in the head knowing he needed all of his concentration on this issue.

Justin slapped the ground as he eked out a, "Marcus."

Marcus began to pick him up, "Justin please reverse this thing."

Justin with his left arm around Marcus's shoulder struggled to press the override code. As he pressed confirm, the engine began to shut down again as the 5 minute timer restarted.

Justin barely said the words, "Over our dead bodies."

Marcus reluctantly nodded, "Exactly."

He held Justin's hand as the strength left his body. Marcus slumped down to the floor and waited there as the clock ticked down, each beep that came every 15 seconds increased his tension. As he waited there, as he felt more exhausted and weaker, the clock hit zero and he let out a sigh of relief as he finally laid down, completely overcome with exhaustion, pain and relief.

Just a few minutes later the reinforcements came down with guns aimed as Marcus pulled himself up. The Major asked him what had happened, Marcus told them everything as the Major nodded. "Soldier, you did well, let's get you to the hospital."

The other soldiers helped him up as he walked through the blood and the bodies lying on the ground. As they walked on he saw Allison dead and the loss truly struck him. He had worked in the same unit as her for a year. The pain of his shoulder and the loss sent tears pouring down his face. They walked him through the control room as he saw the commander being zipped up in a body bag. He was relieved to see that at least Rizalyn had survived.

Marcus called out, "Rizalyn, are the other engines secure?"

She hollered back, "Yes, we were the only ones where they breached the core."

He let out a sigh as they were taking him down Tunnel D to an ambulance. He was just beginning to smile again when they saw a window and he saw the massacre, a field stained red with blood. This wasn't a memorial field, this had just happened as thousands of bodies were still lying there. The smile he had just recovered was lost once again.

He got into the ambulance, as it drove away, one of the medics took his hand, "Thank you so much for everything you have done."

Despite the sincerity, the words seemed to ring hollow, as Marcus said the obligatory, "Thanks, you're welcome." The ambulance was approaching a roundabout when Marcus looked out the window and saw The Natural Way's warped NW logo spray-painted on a wall with the message underneath "It's inevitable." The thought sent chills down his spine.

He was scheduled to come out of the hospital 30 hours later. A military spokesman pulled Marcus aside, "Hello Marcus, I am a military spokesman for the United Planet, my name is Mr. Peabody and I want to start by saying thank you sir for your tremendous dedication and service."

Marcus felt the handshake, as if Mr. Peabody was trying to test his strength. "Marcus, listen when you leave this hospital in a few minutes the media is going to be out there, we have prepared a speech for you."

Marcus feeling like he had been through enough rolled his eyes, "Let me take a look at it."

Mr. Peabody said, "Word has spread that you are a hero, we need you to be a symbol of the immortal human dynasty. Take a few minutes, read it over, say it to the media outside then we'll just get you out of here."

Marcus read the speech and the speech was so rosy and upbeat he wanted to vomit, as if all the death that he saw was being swept under the rug, as if the Natural Way had fully surrendered and nothing like this would ever happen again despite the threat he had seen painted on the wall. With only a few minutes to decide he asked a nurse for a pen and a piece of paper. He came out of the hospital's front door where he was greeted to a hero's welcome, as the media began to bombard him with questions.

Mr. Peabody spoke first, "Marcus has a short speech he would like to give, and then he will be going home to finish his recovery."

Marcus stepped forward as the crowd and the media applauded and put the speech that was written for him away, he had written one of his own. "There are many heroes, I am simply the one of the few who survived. The Natural Way sent roughly 100,000 people at us between the 12 engines and we managed to stop them. However they did reveal something, we aren't there yet; we are still killing each other. A real blood red field with the real blood of real people was created yesterday, and I… lost many friends and colleagues. Today isn't January 2, Year Zero, it is January 2, 2228. Unfortunately the new golden age we have dreamed of, will have to wait. Thank you very much." Marcus gingerly continued walking to the quiet shock of the people who stood around him.

A couple people nervously and intermittently clapped unsure of what was customary in this situation. Once the nervous applause stopped, murmurs buzzed through the crowd seconds later reacting to what Marcus had said.

Mr. Peabody chased after Marcus, he began to reprimand Marcus as the crowd became out of earshot. "What the hell did you just say? That was not the speech I gave you. Do you have any idea the dynamite you just lit?"

Marcus, tired and angry after everything he had been put through went face to face with the spokesman, "What I said is the truth, if you hate me for it, fine."

Mr. Peabody said took a small step back, "Don't you know what we have put into Project Limitless and getting people to believe in Year Zero?"

Marcus got right back in his face, "Year Zero isn't just some PR campaign to make the United Planet's government look good, it's not just a number it is the beginning of a golden age that people since the beginning of civilization have always wanted. I had a lot of time to think while I was in the hospital and I couldn't help but wonder if a truly great new age is possible."

Mr. Peabody became a little disconcerted, "Well of course it is, we are almost there now this little incident was minor setback."

Marcus was disgusted by Mr. Peabody's words, "Minor setback? If you still have an honest bone in your body then tell me Mr. Peabody, is Year Zero an illusion or a dream? If it's an illusion, why are we trying to get to it? If it's a dream, how many more nightmares must we endure before we finally make that dream a reality?"

FOR ALL TIME

My name is Rowan Cleese, I am a 29-year-old man living just outside of Manchester, England, and I live in crazy times, you may be wondering why, if so let me tell you.

It was April 26, 2039 in Switzerland when the first experiment worked, the experiment that started it all. A group of physicists actually sent an insignificant amount of water vapour back in time – 0.87 seconds. On that fateful day, the possibility of going back in time became reality and all of the science fiction 'what ifs' leapt to the front of all the science fiction conventions.

As the 2040's progressed the experiment was peer reviewed, verified and expanded to the point where in early 2049 a lab mouse was sent back in time 2 days. After that everyone wanted to talk about it and the debates became real and heated. It was hard to believe that small riots were happening across Europe, the groups began to unite along two hard lines.

One was called J.F.A.T. or Justice For All Time, the group believed that if we can go back in time and create a better world we should. European history is full of tragic events that we wish had not happened. Almost everyone has one thing or ten in their lives that they wish were different.

The other group was called N.I.T.T. or Non-Interference Time Travellers, they believed that interfering in past events was a formula for disasters and would rather use it the way Charles Dickens did in "A Christmas Carol" as a way to learn from and observe the past. They also asked, "What if someone changes the past for the worse? Who gets access? When does it stop?"

The South London riot of October 2049 brought the topic right to the forefront, a similar riot in Moscow in February 2050 made the topic even more urgent. After all, if you are so ready to fight that you will fight in the streets of Moscow in February then the situation has gotten completely out of hand. In the wake of these disasters a referendum was set, to be called for only the second time in the history of the entire European Union.

It was scheduled for May 18, 2051 with two options, Option 1: *Time Travel will be used to prevent various atrocities for the purpose of a better world.* Option 2: *Time Travel will be limited to purely historical and educational purposes with any interference in past events being strictly illegal.* It almost seemed insane that all of human history could change depending on the will of many millions of people on one day, but there it was and the race was on.

I had a chance to re-watch the "Back to the Future" trilogy, and while the idea of preventing the death of innocent people was tempting, the threat of its misuse was hammered home as well. My brother Simon's birthday almost ended in a fistfight when a bunch of us went out for a few pints only to discover that two of his friends were on opposite sides. It got bad real quick when one of them started getting agitated.

"You damn fool, my father died of cancer, if I can go back in time and stop it from killing him I will and you're not going to stop me."

The other one wasn't much better, "If you go back in time, what's to stop some other wanker from going back to kill people, you stupid bastard."

While we got the situation calmed down, all the ale and lager on earth couldn't keep me from worrying about the consequences no matter which way the vote went.

The televised debates began, while they were a little more thoughtful, it was hard not to sense that they were trying to touch hearts rather than minds. Appealing to fear rather than logic, you don't need to be an expert on history to know that following fear often doesn't end well. While most issues I felt strongly one way or the other, this issue split me in half like a hot knife through butter.

Unfortunately the rhetoric grew stronger and more aggressive with statements like: "If you want us to stand idly by while innocent people by the millions suffer and die, what monster are you?"

The other side would respond with, "Do you want to apply British Law of 2051 to everyone that ever lived? Are you going to take tribal people from 3000 years ago and arrest them? How much of a totalitarian control freak are you?"

It got to the point where I didn't even want to think about it anymore, the vote was just a couple months away and I wanted to think about anything else. Then the ads on the Internet got even blunter and the billboards and posters began appearing everywhere. The ones in Germany were the worst; one would show a picture of the holocaust with the statement "You can stop this, vote option 1 on May 18." The other showed a Nazi rally with the statement "One mistake, and this is our reality, vote option 2 on May 18." For obvious reasons these were controversial, and many justified their side's pandering while declaring the other side as distasteful.

My family's traditional Easter dinner was tense because it was the issue everyone was afraid to mention, even accidentally. While we were having a nice dinner, Simon's girlfriend asked me, "So which way are you votin' May 18?"

I tried to brush it off with humour, "I'm waiting for the me of the future to tell me."

While it did get a mild chuckle from my uncle John, she was having none of it. "Come on Rowan, speak up."

I took a deep breath and gave the only answer I could, "I don't know."

Everyone began to stare as if I just said football wasn't a sport or something.

Simon chimed in, "Oh come on, what's so complicated? Time Travel is dangerous no matter how fun Dr. Who makes it look."

My cousin Meghan suddenly burst, "Are you kidding me you bloody twit? This is easy Rowan, you go back in time and fix mistakes, that is why we have backspace and delete buttons on keyboards."

Simon's girlfriend and cousin Meghan had to be pulled apart within two minutes, nowhere was safe.

It was late April, I was working from home and I had an instant message from my boss. "Did you hear Option 1 is ahead 52 to 47, isn't that great?"

I just went with the only answer I could think of, "We'll see May 18."

By May 5 the polls were saying lots of things, one put Option 1 ahead, another put Option 2 ahead, and others said they were neck and neck. Protests and counter protests were growing and the Prime Minister had to say that the U.K. would be put under martial law if any rioting occurred after the vote. The governments of other European countries had to issue similar ultimatums for their people if there was any trouble.

I couldn't stop worrying, possibly the most important vote in human history and all I could think about was a riot from the losing side. The memories of Simon's birthday and Easter ran through my head. While it had started out as a joke, by this point I really did want the me of the future to tell me what I needed to do, but the future was giving me silence.

With just two days until the vote I was still split right in half, neither made any blockbuster arguments. I began to wonder who I would vote for, word spread that riots were coming either way, I just wanted this nightmare to be over with.

The day of the vote I walked into the polling station almost hoping I would be there to tell me what to do. I finally looked down at the ballot, feeling the weight of the world on my shoulders. The pencil in my hand began to get heavier and heavier. I remembered so many of the things I was told they raced through my head like a runaway train.

I heard one of the administrators ask me, "Is there a problem?"

I said quietly, "No, I'm just about to write it."

She looked at me oddly. I finally looked at a circle not caring which option it supported, wrote my x, folded it up and put it in the ballot box.

I went home, threw on the telly, and watched reruns of some old shows blocking out entirely what was going to happen. Before midnight I heard a bang, and I peered outside seeing people throwing Molotov cocktails. The police arrived it was hard watching this violent brawl just across the street from me. I still didn't know who won the vote, which side these people were on, all I could tell was that they didn't get their way and they were angry as all hell.

I closed my blinds again, just as I did I thought to myself, "What would the time travellers think? Or do?"

I dared to peer out my window again and saw that more police had appeared and had overpowered the rioters on my street. I thought maybe the J.F.A.T. and the N.I.T.T. would do the same thing at this moment observe and learn. As I saw the last one being put in the back of the police car having been beaten during the brawl I wondered what was the point? Why did I vote if it would turn out the same either way? Why couldn't they... use reason and be the bigger people?

I finally realized we don't need to go back in time to change things; there are things to change right now. We don't have to observe the past to learn, we just have to observe now, and there is so much. I realized that this vote led to Martial Law and violence because we had let our worse side take over. The side that believed in winning at all costs as opposed to facing reality with an open mind. I realized if we didn't grow past it, we will be dealing with this today, tomorrow and for all time.

IRRELEVANT

It was another losing month at a big box store, Jacob Malton, a recent university graduate working there on weekends had just been laid off with a few others, such as his older friend Olaf. He walked out of the office when Olaf called out to him, "I'm going for a smoke break, do you want to keep me company?"

Jacob responded, "Sure."

Olaf and Jacob went outside, "They just laid me off. In this economy the only thing I might be able to get is a job flipping burgers and asking people if they want fries with that. I am way smarter than that, maybe if these people listened to the suggestions I made months ago, maybe we wouldn't be struggling right now!"

Olaf spoke up, "Calm down, retail losses in March are standard. What sucks is I got laid off too, and I have a mortgage and two kids to worry about."

Jacob got a spark in his eye, "One day I am going to be the Prime Minister of Canada, and I am going to tell everyone how to do things properly."

Olaf sarcastically responded, "Yeah, good luck with that."

Jacob with his passion and frustration flowing through his veins declared, "If I ran this world, it would be a hell of a lot better."

As Olaf put his cigarette out on the ashtray outside, he dismissively said, "Sure Jacob, whatever you say."

On his way home that evening he walked by a local small electronics store. The TVs in the front showed a terrorist attack that had happened in Moscow leaving 42 dead. He shook his head and went out for a walk. As he walked the gravel path and sat down at the swing set, his thoughts raced.

"I live in one of the greatest countries in the world and life still sucks. If I ran the world things would be better, the economy would be better, wars would be over and graduates like me wouldn't have to worry about their future."

Just as he finished that thought a purple hand with texture like sand paper was placed on his shoulder. Jacob was so shocked he could barely move, when he heard a struggling voice, "Don't be afraid, we are with you."

They were suddenly teleported as Jacob looked around and saw these seven and eight foot tall creatures with rough skin, a head with black eyes and green pupils. Some of this species had purple skin, and some with orange. He looked around confused and frightened, when one in metal shoulder pads and a cape stepped forward, "Welcome, Jacob Malton, we have chosen you for a tremendous honour."

Jacob, though still confused, had focused his confusion, "What honour?" He asked, curious and scared.

"We are the Laquelloste, we are a species that promotes order in the universe. We have found other species like yours and selected good exemplary members and gave the selected remarkable powers so they could be the guardians of their species. With this power you can do things that your species cannot yet, and accomplish great things."

Jacob's mind raced with possibilities, his heartbeat doubled as he became excited. He asked them, "What powers are you giving me?"

The leader of the Laquelloste answered, "You will be able to manipulate molecules at will, teleport anywhere you wish and summon fire, ice, electricity as well as other forces. You will be able to multiply yourself both physically and mentally, putting your consciousness in multiple places at once. With these new powers you will be able to help any of your fellow humans anytime, anywhere because at will you will be able to see and feel what they do."

Jacob was so stunned he had trouble believing that it wasn't a dream. They asked him to step inside a machine on the left side, a thick dark metallic cylinder sticking part way from the wall having various pipes running along the wall fed into it. Jacob approached cautiously as the leader spoke, "Do not be afraid, you will not be harmed, it will give you the power to lead your people to greatness."

Jacob approached the machine as he stepped inside. It was pitch black, he heard a voice from above him, "Take a deep breath, the elements will reach you in one moment."

He began to see small lights coming when several large energy forces hit him at once, as he was shocked and overwhelmed. Electricity flowed between his fingers, his heartbeat was double again what it was and then there was another burst of energy from him in all directions as Jacob fell to his hands and knees.

The door opened and the leader stood there, "How do you feel Jacob Malton?"

Jacob came to his feet slightly dizzy, "This is like nothing I have ever felt before, I feel incredible." The Laquelloste Leader asked him to step out and he did as they walked back to where they were.

The leader continued, "Congratulations, you are now the guardian of your species. Before you begin, take time to get used to your powers so that your efforts to bring greatness to your world are as effective as possible."

Jacob responded, "Thank you, I will never forget this."

The leader stepped away as Jacob was teleported back to earth, to that same park as he looked around and saw no one. Out of curiosity he grabbed one of the metal chains holding his swing and willed it into becoming wood, which it did. He then put it back as it was and walked home.

That night he came home and went straight to his room so he could test his powers further. He laid down on his bed looked up and teleported to the roof, where he began to slide down, and he teleported himself back to his room.

He closed his eyes and concentrated on seeing what his mother saw, as he saw what she was seeing he could hear what she was thinking: "Is Jacob okay? He went straight to his room and barely said a word, I better go up to make sure he's okay." He left her mind as she climbed the stairs, he suddenly remembered that he had been laid off and he would have to tell her that.

She knocked on the door and he came out, he told what had happened and she put her face in her palm. "What are we going to do, you have student loans, I have car payments, and your father is three months behind on alimony."

Jacob gave her a hug, "Don't worry, I will find something better."

Before going to sleep that night he turned on the TV and saw one of the new animated superhero movies. The thought occurred to him, "All I have to do is take care of our money problems, then I can focus all my time on fixing the world's problems."

The next day he concocted a white lie. "If I tell her every day that I am looking for work and then give my mom $600,000 from my dad to stop the alimony payments that will fix everything." He told his father that he had been given the money by a wealthy older man that he had met. Once he assured him that nothing illegal was going on he accepted it and everything was in motion. He knew it would work since his father was never the type that worried much about his kids, his marriage or anything for that matter.

Now with his family's money problems solved he turned his attention to the rest of the world. He thought carefully and realized that he could not reveal himself as himself. He needed something better than a costume, he thought of Dr. Manhattan from Watchmen, if he had a full body force field that looked like someone else, problem solved. He made it green but couldn't resist making it look like a muscular statue. His force field hair would flow down to his shoulders and he gave himself a handlebar moustache that stretched down to his jawline.

He thought of several names, however he decided, "I don't want people thinking of me as God or something like that." He finally settled on the most modest name he could think of "Irrelevant." It had been only a week but he was ready, he could turn on his disguise in an instant, his powers were easier than ever to command and he knew right where to start. He was going to fix the environment, it seemed simple enough, take tonnes of CO2 out of the atmosphere.

Before he started though, he had one huge problem: if he was flying around the sky people might think he was going to do something wrong. He also didn't want any fighter jets coming after him, so he decided that he would reveal his persona to the world. He discovered that a U.N. meeting was scheduled for one week from that weekend, so he practiced his speech over and over. He also did some research about how he could take the excess carbon atoms and turn them into diamonds. There was already a machine that was built to do it. He could just do it bigger and better.

That day he came up with the excuse that he was going to his friend Rod's house, but told his friend Rod he couldn't hang out because he was visiting his Dad. He knew he was about to change the world, the answer to one of its biggest problems and he used his powers to see what was happening as the moment presented itself. He took on his Irrelevant persona and prepared to teleport himself.

He had practiced over and over again, how to maintain the force field without even concentrating and even had prepared his statement in English. However, he was prepared to use the languages in the minds of the other representatives if needed. He was ready, the day humanity would leap forward, the reason…Irrelevant.

He walked into the front door, as the jaws of the representatives hung open in disbelief. The security guards aimed their guns at him, the tension built as everyone was wondering what would happen.

The speech began, "Take my hand, I am your brother, at long last I can help you, I do not want your money, nor do I want your praise, I just ask for your co-operation and willingness to work with me. For centuries man has struggled with issues and prayed for someone to help them, I am the answer to those prayers. I will start with taking the excess carbon dioxide out of the atmosphere, stopping climate change in its tracks, and then I will help with other problems. This is a new era, let's make it a golden one."

He disappeared, teleporting back to his room where he turned on the TV in his room to see the coverage. There was stunned silence as the reporter eked out the words, "I am shocked by what we have just seen and heard. We are waiting for the reaction from various world leaders."

Jacob waited for the different countries reactions; he heard several European countries say that if he is indeed trying to help climate change they would help. Others were less helpful, some were outright antagonistic. Some claimed he was a genetically engineered monster. The North Koreans effectively declared war.

The North Koreans' statement was, "The Supreme Leader fears no one and this green man will be destroyed if he steps foot in this country." Other countries began making demands such as, "We can't let him into this country unless we know who he is and where he lives so he can be arrested."

It had been less than 24 hours and he was more feared than most terrorists. He reluctantly decided to go through with it anyway. The fate of humanity was more important than the egos of insecure dictators. He teleported into the sky and flew around the earth faster than the speed of sound as the collected carbon molecules quickly accumulated behind him. The mass of carbon had become larger and larger, as he continued to change direction to reach different parts of the atmosphere. After several minutes he was hauling tonnes of pure carbon behind him. He stopped over the coast of Norway, he turned around to face the tonnes of pure carbon and willed into becoming perfectly shaped diamonds that could fit in the palm of his hand.

He spoke to the onlookers in their language, "Thank you for your acceptance, here is a sign of my gratitude." The diamonds fell from the sky into the water just off the beach. People looked on in disbelief as he left to continue the removal of carbon atoms. He repeated the diamond dropping off the coasts of other countries whose leaders had been welcoming. After doing this for 11 hours Jacob was feeling tired and went home confident that he had done a wonderful thing.

The next day the news coverage was non-stop, there were complaints, fear, jealousy and threats.

"Why is he taking luxury items and giving them to rich countries, what favouritism." "What is he really doing, what is he putting in the air?"

"Where did this guy get these powers?"

The worst reactions come from the North Koreans, "The green man was warned if he comes over North Korean airspace we will use our missiles to knock him out of the sky. Our Supreme Leader will make an example of this being and show him North Korean power."

That threat was the last straw, he had tried to be nice and now they were threatening to kill him. He was going to show them his power. A few hours they were going to have a rally, as the Supreme Leader stepped forward onto the balcony, "North Korea is the most powerful country in the world, no one will trespass over our land the green man is no match for me. I will protect you." Applause both real and forced rang up from the crowd.

Suddenly a giant green firework shot off over the crowd emerging from it was Irrelevant. He made one full rotation, as all the guns that were pointed at him became piles of sand that fell to the feet of the soldiers.

Irrelevant stared at the Supreme Leader from many feet in the air, his voice rang out in Korean, "I am trying to help all people, since I am leading, and you won't follow then get out of the way! You do not threaten me, your power is nothing compared to mine. All your missiles, nuclear and not are now on a moon rotating Jupiter, as for you," Irrelevant opened a portal that the Supreme Leader fell through and suddenly appeared face to face with Irrelevant, hanging in mid-air.

The Supreme Leader's clothes were telekinetically ripped off and Irrelevant made his hand comically oversized as he repeatedly spanked the Supreme Leader to tears leaving the entire crowd speechless, as he lowered him and left him in the crowd. "Now grow up, I have work to do".

He began flying around again, collecting the carbon out of the atmosphere. He was making his second pass over Russia for the day when a missile exploded just in front of him. He stopped and saw the others coming at him with more concentration they were teleported to the same moon of Jupiter that the North Korean missiles were sent to.

Irrelevant then teleported to the President's office, and began speaking in Russian, "What are you thinking, launching missiles at me?"

The President said, "You declared war on us, you invaded and humiliated the leader of our ally and you stole their weapons. What is to stop you from doing that to us?"

Irrelevant responded, "He threatened me, and I showed him I won't be threatened."

The President responded, "Neither will we, but if you would be willing to do some things to show that you support our national interests we could come to an understanding."

Irrelevant saw through this cheap ploy, "I am giving your offer the cold shoulder," as he put a thick wall of ice over the door. "Stay out of the way and let me do the right thing."

He teleported away picking up where he left off as he continued taking the excess carbon molecules out of the atmosphere and feeling emboldened that he had put the President of Russia in his place.

The United Nations had an emergency meeting with the world leaders and their representatives about the green man. The opinions of representatives from the different countries rang throughout the room, "We supported this being initially, but now that he has crossed lines, this being must be held to account."

"If this being can disable a country's weapons at will, what else is he capable of?"

"This being says he is cleaning our air, what if he is putting something up there that is harmful?"

Irrelevant teleported in, "You all have a lot of nerve giving me all this grief, I have been using my power for two days, I have taken 11 parts per million of carbon out of the atmosphere, more than you have ever done. I have been threatened and assaulted twice, and all I did was spank one leader and inconvenience another. I will accomplish more this year than all of you combined. I used to think you were trying your best, but I now see how incompetent and corrupt you are, so here is how things are going to go: I am going to clean the air and oceans, fighting criminals and terrorists, prevent natural disasters and end war. The rest of you are going to do your part and shut the hell up. Lead, follow or get out of the way, and if you obstruct I will take you out of the way myself. This is your last warning and by the way my name is not the green man, my name is Irrelevant!" Irrelevant teleported away to the shock and dismay of all in attendance, the silence that followed was deafening.

He continued his effort to clean the air, the mood towards him had shifted dramatically, NATO reluctantly sent up fighter jets with C4 charges if they could get close.

Irrelevant was incensed, "I am trying to help you and you are trying to kill me," he thought. "That is it, you asked for it."

The pilots disappeared and the planes were crushed by Irrelevant's powers.

He decided what he would do next, build a prison for those who he was punishing. He used his powers to track down those who had sent the pilots and one by one he had captured them including the Prime Minister of Canada, and the President of the United States among other world leaders.

The world fell from fear into panic, some journalists demanded to speak to Irrelevant. He decided after a few days to oblige and met with them. They asked him, "Are you taking over the world?"

Irrelevant responded, "I am doing what has to be done."

They asked him where he had taken the world leaders and other military personnel. He responded, "Let me show you," and he teleported the dozens of journalists with him to the gate of an underwater prison. "We are in my new prison at the bottom of the ocean, it is protected by a force field that keeps the water out. If anyone comes close to it, I will know."

They stepped into the main hallway. "They are all here."

One of the prisoners was screaming; he had what appeared to be an electric force field around his head, screaming, "I've had enough!" Others were begging, having the same force fields around their heads.

One of the reporters asked, "What are those things around their heads?"

Irrelevant responded, "It triggers the pain centres in the brain, I can give them a 25 year punishment in 6 months. That is their punishment for attempted murder."

One reporter came to the front and her eyes were ablaze with outrage. "So you gave them this punishment without trial, without a legal defense?"

Irrelevant responded, "If you are above the law's restrictions then you are above the law's protection."

The same reporter was undeterred, "Does that apply to you?"

Irrelevant paused, "I suppose so."

The reporter continued, "How does creating a two tier system help? It creates a world of 'might makes right' which is a world that is indefensible. You exacting your will on others, without oversight or accountability isn't making the world better, it has created a piece of hell on earth."

Irrelevant had heard all that he could stand, and proclaimed, "Enough," and glared back. "You short-sighted imbeciles, have bothered me enough," and they were all teleported back.

Irrelevant went home after another hard day, and he was relaxing in his room when his mother came home. She called up to him as he came down the stairs, "Jacob, I need to talk to you for a minute."

He rolled his eyes, "Yes mom, what is it?"

"Honey I need to talk to you."

He responded, "Okay mom I am listening. What is it?"

She responded, "I am really scared."

He looked confused, "What about?"

She continued, "Irrelevant, that green monster, there is no telling what he will do next and I would hate for you join one of these anti- Irrelevant militias and get yourself put in one of those torturous prisons or killed."

Jacob tried to defend Irrelevant, "Didn't the people he imprison try to kill him?"

She looked at him, "Honey, power corrupts and absolute power corrupts absolutely. I would give anything to go back to the way things were."

Jacob was confused, "But hasn't he been cleaning the air, hasn't he been trying to do the right thing, hasn't he saved cities from storms?"

His mother burst into tears and threw her arms around him, "Honey, it's not worth it, this thing will destroy everything in its path. If Irrelevant has already gone this far in a week, what about a month, a year, or a decade? Honey I am sorry you will have to live the rest of your life in a world like this." She wept with her arms around her son.

While the words of the reporter were sharp, these hit him so much harder as he struggled with what he had done and he wondered if everyone felt the way his mother did. He went up to his room as he looked at his hands, wondering if all that power was in the right hands.

He put his consciousness in the minds of the prisoners of his prison and he felt their relentless agony. He stopped as tears formed in his eyes, second-guessing himself for the first time. He decided to push his powers to the limit and he was going to reach everyone. His concentration grew exponentially, he felt the emotions of people all over the world; anger, fear, envy but the emotion that stabbed his heart like a knife was hopelessness.

He felt the people losing hope by the second; everything he had done was meaningless, all they could think about was their hopelessness in the face of his seemingly unstoppable power. The feeling that everything they wanted for their loved ones and themselves would be destroyed. He left their minds looking at his hands once again wondering if his hands were the right ones. Were all those millions of people being short-sighted or was he?

He got out of his bed and looked out his window to the people walking down the street and he felt their pain, their stress and their heartbreak. He wrote a note to his mother explaining everything, which he titled, "Doing the right thing."

He became Irrelevant once again and freed his prisoners, he felt their relief and confusion.

"Why?" one of the generals asked

"I was wrong." He returned them to where he had picked them up and he said, "farewell."

He took a deep breath, knowing what he was about to do, what had to be done and he used his powers to launch himself towards the sun. Even at his close to top speed it took several minutes, his force field protected him, he was ready to drop it as soon as he made contact with the sun. The moment finally came; the light overwhelmed then he felt cold and then nothing.

He woke up on a metal table looking at a set of purple lights several feet above him, like the ones on an operating table. He looked to the left seeing the Laquelloste behind a glass window. Before he could fully comprehend what had happened a screen turned on to his right.

"Attention Jacob Malton, you have just been through the Laquelloste endowment test. Based on our criteria, you have failed and other humans will be considered for this test."

Utterly confused he was trying to fully understand what happened, "Wait, wait has everything for the last few weeks been a dream?"

The screen continued, "We wish you well. You will now be returned to earth."

While still trying to figure out what had happened he was suddenly back on the swing set, he tried to will the swing set chain to becoming wood, and nothing happened. He walked home, looking at the night sky, he saw a newspaper box and it was still the day he had been laid off. He went home thinking about everything that had happened trying to figure out how much of it was real, if any of it.

Before he walked up to his door he heard a yell from somewhere down the street, "You orange and purple bastards, give them back! I want those powers back!"

While Jacob was initially relieved that he hadn't simply lost his mind, his door closed and the reality of the situation hit him.

The next day he went to Todd's house, and as they began to talk about the usual topics, Todd interrupted him. "I need to tell you something, top secret, not…a…soul." Jacob agreed. "This morning I was kidnapped by orange and purple aliens calling themselves the Laquelloste and they went in my head."

Jacob cut him off, "I know, it happened to me last night."

"What?" Todd's jaw almost fell off his face "So they are really looking to give those powers to someone?" Todd asked.

"I guess so," Jacob answered.

"How did you do?" Todd asked

"Let me put it this way, I quit after a few weeks. What about you?" Jacob asked

"I'd rather not say," Todd responded.

There was a long difficult pause with a question on the tip of Todd's tongue that finally leapt off "So who do you think will get the powers?"

Jacob felt the urge to respond, "I don't know, it depends on what the Laquelloste are looking for. All they told me was 'greatness'. They never told me anything else, anything specific."

"Do you think they are looking for someone who won't go too far, or misuse the powers?" Todd asked with desperation.

"I don't know, if they are I'm not sure anyone will get the powers."

Todd looked at him confused, "Why?"

Finally the question that had haunted Jacob came forth, "Are there any people that wouldn't misuse absolute power, is anyone incorruptible?"

Another long pause followed. "We might find out if they pick somebody." Todd continued, "My uncle Jerry is kind of cynical, he always says that 'people suck, that's why the world sucks' what if he's right?"

Jacob said, "Maybe, but I guess that's why no one should have too much power. Maybe it doesn't matter who gets the powers, because the dictator's name is always Irrelevant."

BRING THE KIDS TO LEARNING LAND

It was another day in suburbia; the 14-year-old daughter Monica was grounded for bringing home poor grades and the 10-year-old son Ronnie was on the Internet talking to his friends about the new video games coming out soon. As always the parents were miserable, having yet another fight.

"Maybe you should spend more time with Monica, right now her best grade is a C minus."

The Father responded, "You know I don't have time. Maybe if I hadn't married you out of high school I wouldn't have to work 2 jobs to pay for Ronnie's blow-shit-up game."

The wife rolled her eyes, "Well pardon me for trying to give our kids something better than what we had."

The husband responded, "If you want them to have it better, tell Ronnie not to fall for the first easy girl that comes around."

The wife grabbed the lamp and threw it against the wall forgetting that Monica could hear all of it. As usual Monica tried to block it out by watching TV, then she heard her parent's bedroom door slam shut.

Her mother walked in a moment later saying that she had to talk to Monica about her grades, Monica said that she wasn't interested. Her mother's anger began to rise again, "Look Monica, you and your generation have no idea how good they have it. You live in the greatest country in the world and have opportunities other people can't dream of. I'm not letting you throw that away, so stop watching TV and start studying."

Just before her mother could grab the remote an ad came on for the brand new amusement park, "Learning Land, where education meets excitement."

The light bulb went off over her mother's head, "That looks like fun! All four of us can go. It will be great for everyone."

Monica rolled her eyes, "Will Dad have time, and can we go to this place without you lecturing me on and on?"

Her mother got upset, "That's the problem with your generation, you have no respect for anything and you want everything handed to you. We're going to Learning Land next Saturday and we are going to be one big happy family."

She walked out as Monica thought to herself, "Who is she trying to convince, me or her?"

The night before the trip Monica and Ronnie had ordered a pizza because their father was working late and their mother was away grocery shopping. Monica asked Ronnie what he thought about going to Learning Land tomorrow, his response was, "It looks lame, like one of those amusement parks that tries to be cool and just fails...hard."

Monica nodded in approval, thinking about how school was just a responsibility with seemingly no real reward. Monica said to Ronnie, "When I get grounded again can I borrow your spare headphones?"

Ronnie looked at her and said, "Okay but you owe me."

Monica thanked him with pity, not for herself but for him; how much longer until they treat him the way her parents treated her?

The next morning they woke up at 7 am, so they could leave by 8 am and they could get there right at 10 am when the park opened. The car ride was awkward between the four of them, the mother broke the ice telling them that this is what being a family is all about: learning things together as a family. Monica foresaw this as just another chore that her parents were cramming down her throat, maybe if she kept Ronnie out of trouble they would finally let her off of being grounded so she could spend time with her friends.

The line up to get in was about 20 minutes, so they began to look around and they saw one of the park's mascots in a costume, Ollie the Orangutan who had glasses and was dressed up like a professor.

Ronnie blurted out, "Look a Disney reject, I wonder what other retarded stuff is here."

Their mother's temper was already short and she got mad at him, "Don't talk like that, this is a great place and you are going to shut up, learn and like it."

Monica began to stare at another family that looked like they were getting along, Monica looked on thinking, "Why couldn't I be part of that family?"

As the day progressed, they passed by the carnival games that were math based. Monica began to have her interest peaked in the aquarium, she was amazed at the descriptions of some of the creatures. Ronnie's complaining began to push his parents over the edge, seeing this and wanting to keep the peace Monica asked Ronnie to come with her to go on some rides. She and Ronnie walked away when she was beginning to hear all of the familiar bickering.

"He gets this from you, you're not satisfied with anything either."

They found a roller coaster called "Velocity," Ronnie let out a big, "Finally, something fun!"

As they waited in line the video screen overhead was teaching physics, explaining velocity, acceleration and momentum. Finally they got on the ride, as they heard the voice over the speakers, "On this ride, velocity plus acceleration and changing altitudes equals…awesome."

For the first time that day, a bright smile came across Monica's face as the thrill of this ride filled her with adrenaline. The ride briefly slowed down across a turn and she saw a large jet-black, three-storey building that peaked her interest.

She asked about the building and had to talk Ronnie into going with her. "Look, I have a feeling it is something amazing in that building, if you go with me to it, we'll do whatever you want for the rest of the day."

Ronnie agreed as they asked for directions and finally approached the building, it looked out of the way with a winding path that people didn't seem to notice. All that was there on the beginning of the path was a sign: "Follow this twisted road to the hall of horrors… Warning: not intended for small children."

With that sign she looked at Ronnie and in a teasing tone asked, "Well, do you want to go in or are you scared?"

Ronnie began to talk back, "I'm not scared of anything, and I bet it won't even be that scary, they'll probably be telling us how bad cavities are."

They followed the winding downward path, with the occasional warning sign saying things like "Beware what lies inside, you will never be the same." Each dare made both of them continue towards it surer that the dares were a bluff.

The winding path took them about a minute and a half to get through as they finally approached the intimidating three-storey building. They finally got there as they looked at each other and opened the thick wooden door with "Hall of Horrors" carved into it. As they walked in the narrow hallway took a left turn, they turned the corner to see a full sized talking Dracula saying in the stereotypical Dracula voice, "Bleh…what you will see is far scarier than me."

They stepped on the rectangle carpet as the door opened and they stepped in and saw a graphic depiction of African slavery. These mannequin sized dolls looked so lifelike, seeing the whipping, the burning and the quiet screaming.

Monica said, "I think we should go," only to turn around and see the thick door had closed and locked behind them. The door had a sign with the thick red letters saying, "They couldn't go back and neither can you." As they realized they couldn't hide from this, they watched these depictions as the plaques on the wall proclaimed that these went on for centuries and this happened to millions of people all over the world. After seeing the depictions of the black people who had been hanged for trying to vote in the 20th century they finally reached the door that opened as they stepped on the carpet.

Ronnie blurted out the obvious, "That's screwed up."

They then found a set of narrow winding stairs that went up as the door closed behind them saying again that they couldn't go back, "The only way out is up."

As Monica climbed the stairs having a hard time imagining having to live under such conditions, she saw the decaying bodies of migrating natives as the wall proclaimed what had happened in the 1830's in the event called "The Trail of Tears." This was shorter but still very disturbing, the decomposing child left Monica with a tear in her eye and left Ronnie speechless as they finally reached the next door, wondering what other horrible things they would be subjected to.

As they stepped into the next door and it closed and locked behind them. They looked to the right and saw a crowd pointing their fingers at a woman, and they looked to the left and saw a rotating stake in the ground and they saw a life size doll in increasing stages of being burned alive. The plaque on the wall explained the event of the Salem witch trials, she looked back at the first girl who was being accused and saw this innocent person who reminded her of herself, being burned alive because of paranoia and greed.

They went through the next door with reluctance and dread, wondering how they could take much more. But in the next room they saw the internment of Japanese civilians during World War II. At least the bloodshed wasn't there, they had seen enough corpses for a whole year and then they were shown the depictions of the people who were burned alive by fire-bombing both in Japan and in Dresden Germany. It was gruesome and stomach churning; the flesh melting off their bodies was almost more than they could take. The worst part was seeing this and knowing this was no movie – this really happened.

As much as this disgusted them, they couldn't help but look at this carnage behind the glass. They finally approached the next door which led to another narrow winding staircase upwards, with a sign once again saying, "The only way out is up." They went up knowing that they couldn't go back and no exit was in sight. Next they saw what happens to a person when you drop napalm and Agent Orange, such as were dropped in Vietnam. By this point Monica and Ronnie were so traumatized, they believed that hell couldn't be worse than this. As usual the facts and statistics were posted on the wall and the sheer numbers were simply overwhelming.

When they reached the next door hoping that this nightmare would be over soon, they looked through and saw models of neighbourhoods in the 1970s and saw those same neighbourhoods represented today, as the descriptions explained the jobs that had been exported destroying the bargaining power of workers. How recent this was stunned her as she looked at the final statistic explaining the exploding cost of college and the size of student loans. The final thing they saw before the door was a casket with the appearance of a middle-aged man in it. There was a piece of paper on top of it stating that this person is one of thousands who died every year for decades because they did not have health insurance.

The door opened as they hoped that this nightmare was finally over but they found more depictions of the tortures done at Guantanamo Bay. Discomfort didn't begin to describe what Monica and Ronnie were feeling. As they read the description of waterboarding, realizing it had been done in their short lifetimes, it chilled them. They finally made it through the next door and they saw a staircase, a narrow winding staircase heading downward. Disturbed beyond belief Monica just wanted to get out of this terrible place. As she made it down the two flights of stairs with Ronnie, she turned the corner and saw the final door with a message that stunned her at her core.

After they got out they went back into the park and they saw their parents walking by. As Ronnie ran up to them, talking a mile a minute about what he had seen, their parents were horrified beyond belief. They marched up to Monica, "What are you telling this child?"

She proceeded to say, "It wasn't me, it was the hall of horrors building. It sure was one."

The parents were especially incensed when Ronnie asked, "Why were we waterboarding people?"

Their parents were ready to have a fit, "Monica go buy your brother a snack, here is $10. We're going to talk to the man who owns this park about this hall of horrors."

Their parents came up to one of the cotton candy sellers and they demanded to know where the owner was, he gave them directions to the office. They got there and had to wait ten minutes.

Finally the owner came out as pleasant as could be, asking, "So what can I do for you today?"

The father blurted out, "Don't give me this nice crap, we paid to get in and another $5 to park, only to find out that you are telling our children a bunch of anti-American propaganda."

The owner looked at them and said, "What are you referring to?"

The mother spoke up, "Don't play dumb with us. Your hall of horrors has our son asking about our country committing war crimes. America doesn't do that; we raise our children to love their country."

The owner took a deep breath as he tried to explain it to these dense people. "First of all, we are an educational park, and that includes history and history is sometimes unpleasant."

The father then added on, "Well why are you saying all this stuff our country did, what about the terrible stuff Germany did? Do you hate our country?"

The owner said, "Actually I do love our country despite its mistakes, because I think loving a country is like loving a person; if you don't really know them can you really love them?" The owner picked his cell phone out of his pocket, "I'm sorry I have a meeting in a few minutes, thank you for coming and I hope you enjoyed the rest of the park."

He shook the father and mother's hands as he quickly walked away. The father and mother tried to look but not stare at each other as they began to remember that their wedding was only 8 months after their first date.

On the way home, the father and mother were speechless. Ronnie had his face buried in his video game but Monica was looking at her cell phone reading the picture she had taken of the message painted on the final door of the hall of horrors. This wasn't just another picture to her, she was planning to keep this picture saved and archived for the rest of her life. A picture that may have answered a question she had asked herself at various times in her life.

"This building cost $11.6 million to build; let's put an end to the torture, killing and exploitation so we don't have to add additional exhibits and you don't have to explain to future generations how your generation failed as every generation did before them."

TWISTED AND TRAUMATIZED

It seemed like just another day on the Chicago police force, when Sargent Jermaine Mordon was called into the Lieutenant's office. The name card on the front of the desk of Lieutenant Winslow was usually a sign of humour or a sign of fear depending on who you asked and when.

"Sargent Mordon, thank you for coming, please sit down. Listen, I have this new kid named Michael Pratt coming in from DeKalb, he went through the academy, and he only has about two months of experience which is why I want you to mentor him and show him how to do things right."

Jermaine tried to contain his annoyance, "Okay sir, whatever you say."

Lieutenant Winslow saw through it, "Look I know you liked your routine, you and Hernandez were a great team but he got injured on the job and now is the opportunity to make another great cop for the team."

Jermaine held his tongue, not wanting to set off Lieutenant Winslow's fuse, "Yes sir, I will start molding as soon as I meet him."

A satisfied grin came across the Lieutenant's face, "Great he will be here in an hour. You and him will be out on patrol, make sure he watches everything you do and learns to do it right."

Jermaine said, containing his annoyance, "Don't worry I will, he will learn the procedures and do everything right."

After he left the office, all Jermaine could think about was, "This kid came from a small place like DeKalb, this is Chicago this is where the streets can get mean and tough and this kid only has two months of low level experience?"

Jermaine was dreading this chore and disappointed that he wasn't going to be paired up with a police officer that already knew what they were doing. However a good police officer does the best they can with whatever cards they are dealt.

As Jermaine was finishing some leftover paperwork from yesterday, officer Chan tapped him on the shoulder, saying, "There he is."

Jermaine looked up to see a guy who looked like he was 22-years-old even though his file said he was 26, and appeared to have no rough edges at all like he had no idea what he was in for. Jermaine walked up and introduced himself, Michael Pratt introduced himself saying it was an honour to serve with Chicago's finest and that he was especially honoured to be working with an officer who had served for over 10 years who had two commendations to his name. While Jermaine was initially surprised he brushed it off in his own mind: "He did his homework, but he will need a hell of a lot more than that, these streets will eat this kid alive."

Jermaine showed him around taking him through various procedures, where to deposit paperwork, evidence and so on. Jermaine continued, "And coming around the corner is one of the most important pieces of equipment that every police station must have in order function properly… the coffee maker." A mild grin came across his face as he said that, remembering his early days on the force. "Do you drink coffee Michael?"

Michael responded, "No."

Jermaine responded, "Trust me, after a year and a few sleepless nights this machine will be one of your best friends."

After walking him through some of the basics, they were going to head out on patrol for the afternoon. Jermaine led him outside, "Here are the police cars, we will be heading out on patrol shortly. Remember that when we go out there, you will see things you didn't see in DeKalb, Chicago can be a great place, but with every big place the greats are greater but the mean streets get meaner."

Just before they got in the car, Michael said, "Hey can I take a picture with you and the car? It's not going on Facebook or anywhere online, I just want it for my house."

Jermaine responded with a shrug, "What the hell."

Michael's enthusiasm was almost infectious and he couldn't help but crack a smile as the picture was taken. As they got in the car Jermaine decided to asked him what was on his mind, "Now that no one is around I'm going to tell you this straight up, I don't see you as a cop, I don't see any rough edges, you look like you just finished university and you've seen nothing. I need to know something, what is the worst thing you saw when you were on duty in DeKalb?"

Michael's demeanour changed as his bright smiling face turned into a look of contemplation, "It was about a month ago, my partner and I came onto the scene of a car accident. Some drunk driver who hadn't buckled in had driven off the road crashed into a light post and went through the windshield." Michael looked at him, "Why, don't you think I can make it?"

Jermaine looked on, "I see you walking in almost smiling like a goof. Okay so you have seen some stuff but what you saw that night is just the beginning. If we get some real deep shit, I don't know if you will be able to handle it, a lot of people can't, I have seen a lot of people who couldn't cut it."

Michael looked back at him, "I got this, believe me I want to be a police officer. I am going to make a difference and that is why I don't need coffee, I look in the mirror, see me in the uniform and that is all I need."

As the car pulled out of the parking lot Jermaine responded, "We'll see."

The next day, Jermaine and Michael were on patrol when some woman ran in front of their car talking a mile a minute. "He's in there, he's got a gun, and I heard him shoot it!"

Jermaine and Michael told her to calm down and take some deep breaths and as soon as she composed herself she explained that up ahead was a man holding people hostage inside of Burger Buster. Jermaine began, "Miss, please wait here by the bus stop, we will get control of the situation. But we will need your statement once the situation is under control okay?"

She nodded, Jermaine went over to the radio, "We have a hostage situation, at the Burger Buster on Bayside just south of Valley; please send backup."

The radio responded, "Copy that."

Michael paused, "Wait a minute, we don't need to wait for backup, there are two of us, one of him and we can get the element of surprise."

Jermaine paused, "What are you talking about?"

Michael continued, "I worked in one of these places once, and they are all set up almost exactly the same, follow me." Michael headed over to the building as Jermaine reluctantly followed him.

Jermaine caught up to him as they reached the back area of the Burger Buster. Jermaine put his hand on his shoulder, "The surveillance camera."

Michael responded, "He's watching them not the camera."

They opened the door and crawled along the floor. There was silence as they poked their heads around the corner, seeing the hallway leading to the cash registers where the armed man was looking at all of the hostages who he had positioned in front of the front windows. Michael and Jermaine crawled across the ground watching for the slightest movement from the gunman. Jermaine began to crawl to the right side of the counter as Michael grabbed a random box of fries that had hit the ground and threw it over the counter to the gunman's left. As the gunman looked to his left to see what had hit the ground Michael leapt up and grabbed him, as the gunman was struggling free Jermaine took him down from behind, took the gun from his hand and held him down with a knee to the neck.

The people began to applaud as Jermaine and Michael picked the guy up and Jermaine began reading the gunman his rights. The other police cars arrived as they were taking the man out of the restaurant, Michael and the other police officers began to get statements from the various hostages. As Jermaine finished reading the man his rights he looked back and saw people hugging Michael, thankful to have been freed and he thought, "It turned out really well, I wonder if he knows how lucky he is."

Later that night Michael and Jermaine were called into Lieutenant Winslow's office, Michael looking at his name tag tried to hold back a chuckle. "What's so funny there rookie?"

Michael began, "Sorry sir, it's just your last name is Winslow and-"

Jermaine cut him off, "Stop, just stop."

The Lieutenant told them both to sit down, "Jermaine, I told you to teach him the right way, the right way does not include playing hero. What the hell were you two thinking?"

Michael looked at Jermaine as if for guidance but began on his own, "I thought that if 10 police cars showed up, the situation would be much more tense and the guy might try and shoot people to show he was serious. I worked in a Burger Buster in DeKalb so I knew how to get into the place and how the back area would be formatted. We had a witness saying it was only one gunman, so combining our knowledge of the inside with the element of surprise I thought we could stop the gunman before anyone was harmed and it went according to plan."

The Lieutenant rolled his eyes, "Listen kid, that's about the best answer that you could have come up with but it was still wrong. If that gunman had heard you coming or just turned his head the wrong way and saw you, chaos would have broke out, that wasn't a plan kid, you were just plain lucky."

Jermaine was frozen in his chair fearing suspension or some other long-term punishment. Michael paused, "Please don't blame Jermaine, it was my idea, he was trying to mitigate my behaviour. I think it would be in the best interest of the police force not to suspend us because if we are being called heroes, it would reflect badly on the precinct and on you specifically."

The Lieutenant looked at him in disbelief, "Jermaine, I think you forgot to tell him that I don't like smart mouths, especially when they talk back to me, take unnecessary risks or who chuckle at my last name. You are lucky that your little hero stunt didn't hurt anyone, you are damn lucky that the media are calling you two heroes and not reckless, and you are really damn lucky that Jermaine has such a clean record and you are new. If you ever pull any crap like this again, your luck will run out do I make myself clear?"

Jermaine said, "Yes sir."

"Yes sir," Michael responded.

The Lieutenant concluded by declaring, "Good. Get out of my office."

Before they left the office Michael sarcastically blurted out, "He's pleasant."

Jermaine said, "Now do you see why we have rules, I went along with you and I almost got suspended. I have a wife and kids to care for, do everything by the book from now on." Jermaine walked out as Michael looked at him confused, feeling like he and the rest of the police station had different missions.

The next day they were called into Lieutenant Winslow's office. "Gentlemen sit down. Alright, Thursday night a woman named Sandra Matelli disappeared outside the Pain & Gain Gym, Jermaine, I know you want this kid to get up to speed so take him to see this, look everything over and get him to do a proper report."

Jermaine nodded, "And you Michael, no heroics, stay by the book."

Michael nodded, "Yes sir".

At the Pain & Gain Gym they spoke to the owner, Mr. Wells, who showed them the surveillance footage. What was so hard to tell was that the attacker was wearing a faded brown hood and was purposely keeping his face or even chest out of view of the camera. Michael began asking questions, "How long has she been coming here?"

Mr. Wells said, "About three years, she was very active, she was a regular at our Thursday night aerobics classes."

They couldn't see which vehicle took her away, she was simply overpowered, smothered with what looked like a chloroform rag and dragged away. Jermaine and Michael asked a few of the other gym members if they had seen or heard anything suspicious but nothing at all came up.

Jermaine and Michael began the drive back to the precinct, "Okay Michael, I'm going to ask you a few questions and I'm going to find out if you were paying attention."

Michael responded, "Okay."

The questioning began: "What did the reaction of the gym people indicate?"

Michael responded, "That they didn't know her very well, which means that whatever friends she had weren't there."

Jermaine asked, "What did the owner's reaction indicate?"

Michael responded, "He didn't seem to care too much, which means he had no personal connection and this is just a business to him and nothing more."

Jermaine continued, "What did the surveillance tape show?"

Michael responded, "There was no wasted movement and impeccable timing; the guy is either lucky as hell or far more likely, this was premeditated and he chose that particular victim for a specific reason."

Jermaine nodded, "Very good, what is the next step?"

Michael responded, "We have to talk to her family and friends to look for anything suspicious, and we may even need to look for surveillance cameras in the adjacent buildings to see which vehicle took her away and when."

Jermaine nodded, "Very good, we're going to her home now, hopefully her husband will know something."

They got to her house and the husband was deeply upset, "Where is she?"

Jermaine said, "We need you to answer some questions, so we can piece this thing together."

The husband got even madder, "You better not be bullshitting me, she means everything to me, she has been gone for over 36 hours."

Michael responded in a serious, frustrated tone, "Look, we understand, I am going to work overtime on this case, but if you want to give her the best chance you can, you need to calm down and answer some questions."

The husband got defensive, "What do you think, I did it?"

Michael sternly responded, "That is not what we are saying, but you're not helping your wife by yelling at us. So calm down, answer the questions so we can move onto the next step of our investigation."

The husband relented, "Fine, she went out for her aerobics classes on Thursday nights, then she would go out with her friends to the bar. She would come home late because she was blowing off steam, so it wasn't until her friend Cassidy called at 10 pm asking why she never showed up that I began worry."

Jermaine continued, "Did she ever mention anyone that she might have been worried about, an ex-boyfriend, a co-worker she had issues with, some family member she didn't get along with?"

The husband said, "No, she pretty much kept to herself. I don't know how I am going to raise these kids, they are really scared and I don't know what to say to them."

Jermaine gave Michael a look of, "Do you see this?"

They left promising to explore further.

As they got into the car Jermaine asked Michael, "What do you think of what you just heard?"

Michael responded, "They were having issues and he is trying to pretend the issues don't exist to keep us from looking at him. As Shakespeare would say,

I think he dos' protest too much."

Jermaine said, "You catch on quick, there might be hope for you yet."

They went over to her friend Cassidy's apartment and began asking her questions. "Did she ever express any concern over any ex-boyfriends, possible stalkers, or anyone like that?"

Cassidy let out a chuckle, "Concern? She was so tired of her husband that she was one big fight away from jumping on the first guy she could. That marriage was going downhill quick and she told me over and over how much she wished she was as free as Gloria and I are. I even saw her making out with a few guys a couple of weeks ago, now that I think about it one of the only guys she ever said was getting too close was the owner of the gym, Mr. Wells. He's one of those guys that you can tell doesn't get it very often and we almost left the gym because he wouldn't back off."

Jermaine looked at Michael taking notes, thinking that they were getting on the same page as far as this case. They drove back to the station to finish their shift as Jermaine quizzed Michael again, "Okay, based on what we have seen and heard, what do you think is the correct course of action?"

Michael responded, "A bar is a public place and people don't always respond to cheating well, not to mention I think it is suspicious that the husband didn't call the police even after Cassidy called."

Jermaine continued, "Okay, do you see other possibilities?"

Michael responded, "Another likely scenario is that maybe the husband knew about her cheating but was looking the other way for the kids. Maybe Mr. Wells is it, he would know exactly where the cameras are and it would explain why he was showing so little interest to us, when he apparently showed more to Sandra."

Jermaine continued, "Exactly, tomorrow we hit both areas harder, since both have the means and the motive."

The next day they walked into work when Lieutenant Winslow called them into the office and said, "Men, this kidnapping case has just gone up a notch: Cassidy, the woman you took a statement from yesterday evening, was spotted being grabbed into a van outside Muldoon's pharmacy this morning. I want a full report on my desk this evening. When you get that footage I want you to run the plates, vehicle history, and I want to know who put the bumper on before it left the factory. Are we clear men?"

They both responded, "Yes sir."

They obtained the footage, spoke to the witnesses including the pharmacist who said, "Yes, Cassidy came in here almost every Sunday morning. She often spoke of getting either painkillers for her hangover or more contraceptives, she wasn't a private person by any means."

They reviewed the surveillance footage repeatedly, and they saw something similar, quick, no waste in movement and efficient. They found out that the vehicle was a brown van but looked like it had some spots on it that looked green and another little bit that looked yellow, indicating that it had been re-painted on a few occasions. The plates were clever forgeries that were not assigned to a particular vehicle.

They then went to speak to the other two women who Sandra and Cassidy had frequently hung out with. Gloria was first, "I think her husband did it, I mean word can spread real quick in this day and age I think he heard about her looking for some thrills on the side and went off. As for Cassidy, she was the party girl of our group, I think he figures she got into her head and maybe he hates her too, all I know is I am looking over my shoulder."

They then spoke with Theresa, "The four of us became friends in the aerobics classes. We were roughly the same age and we were all trying to get in shape, I never met Sandra's husband but I did hear about what was going on, and I didn't want to nag but I told Sandra on a couple of occasions that if you can't work it out just divorce him."

The case seemed to be pointing directly at Sandra's husband. After doing a little further background check, they found out that he had been a manager at a rent-a-car place for five years and had only just started his new position a month earlier at a repair garage, a job where he could get access to many vehicles and might know how to make counterfeit license plates. All of this was detailed in the report for Lieutenant Winslow, the report's conclusion was a warrant to search their home and the repair garage he worked at.

The following day was a Monday and several police officers appeared on the scene of Mr. Matelli's work. Jermaine whispered to Michael, "You be the bad cop."

Jermaine and Michael pulled Mr. Matelli into a private room, Jermaine began, "Mr. Matelli is there anything you want to tell us that you forgot to on Saturday?"

Michael interjected with disdain, "Like maybe you thought your wife was having, or planning to have an affair and you hated her for it?"

Mr. Matelli paused, "Okay, okay, I heard that she was going to clubs and making out with other guys, but I wasn't going to hurt her. I was fighting with myself about getting a divorce or taking her for marriage counselling. We have kids, I don't want to put them through a divorce, they shouldn't be put in the middle of that crap."

Michael got very heated, "You didn't want to make the kids suffer, so you didn't call the cops when their mother was missing, what the hell are your priorities?"

Jermaine put his hand on Michael's chest, "Easy, sorry about him he's new. Mr. Matelli, we saw a large brown van at the scene that looked like it had been painted and it had counterfeit license plates. Considering your automobile knowledge that seems a little too convenient."

Mr. Matelli stared in anger and disbelief, "Convenient, is that all you care about? My wife and her slutty friend are missing and your first thought is 'Oh her husband did it'? You two can go"

Michael cut him off, "I'll come back here when I'm off duty and meet you outside if you want to go, pal. Look up some damn statistics, it usually is the person close to them in their lives. You already hid stuff from us once, why should we believe you're sincere now?"

Jermaine had to calm the situation down, "Everyone, everyone, let's not lose sight of why we are here. Mr. Matelli is there anything else you can tell us?"

He responded, "I'm getting a lawyer, if you break anything at my work or my house I will sue you into the ground!"

On Michael's face was a look that could kill.

Jermaine and him met outside with the other police officers who had conducted the search, "Nope, nothing."

They went over to the radio, "Anything at his house?"

The other officers responded, "Nothing, no sign of anyone or anything."

Michael let out a, "Damn it," before they got back in their cars to head back to the precinct. Jermaine asked Michael, "Were you a little too into being the bad cop back there?"

Michael responded with visceral disgust, "Guys like that who hide behind kids just make me sick."

Jermaine responded, "You need to work on that, this badge isn't just a symbol of the shield we put up between the good people and the criminals, it's a shield for how you keep your personal feelings and biases out of your work."

Michael continued, "I can't wait to nail that guy."

Jermaine responded, "Well, keep your eyes on the right path and if we get the evidence we need, we will."

After they got back in the station they assigned a couple of police officers each to protect Gloria and Theresa as well as a police car to watch Mr. Matelli. Jermaine began heading home when he saw Michael still working. "Michael, its 6 pm you were only scheduled for an 8 hour shift."

Michael looked up at him from the computer screen, "When the criminals agree to work 7 I'll think about it. I am going to solve this case, if I don't get Mr. Matelli I will get whoever it is."

Jermaine shook his head, "Michael, look up." Jermaine put his arm around him and began pointing to different people in the room. "Divorced, separated, happily married as far as he tells us, divorced, single, single, divorced, you are a young guy, don't burn yourself out."

Michael began to get confused, "I thought we were the Chicago PD, serve and protect?"

Jermaine pulled out his wallet, "Do you know why I serve and protect?"

He showed Michael a picture of his family. "This right here. If I spend too much time at the office if I let this job consume me, I lose this, if I lose this you may as well kill me."

Michael paused, "I think I know what you're saying, let me finish what I'm looking up and I will be out of here in half an hour, maybe 45 minutes."

Jermaine nodded, "Okay, we got a tough day ahead of us tomorrow."

The next day Jermaine and Michael met in the locker room and Jermaine asked, "So Michael what did that extra research tell you?"

Michael's frustration began to emerge, "I'm starting to think it wasn't Mr. Matelli."

Jermaine asked, "What makes you think that?"

Michael responded, "A couple things, for starters, for someone who should have a great knowledge of the automobile industry, those were shabby paint jobs."

Jermaine paused, "What else?"

Michael continued, "According to a follow up question from the girls, Sandra had been going to the bar with them for girl's night for years but only started flirting with other guys a couple months ago, and the making out incident only happened 3 weeks ago. For that short of a timespan it seems too precise, especially taking the camera angles and timing into account. So I started thinking again about the gym owner. Not only does his gym location have a big storage area, big enough to get a van in and out of but, he goes to that pharmacy a lot buying supplements and other things. So he may have had the place scoped out, and had the perfect place to hide when the first kidnapping happened."

Before Jermaine could fully process what he had heard, Officer Chan walked in with a deeply saddened look on his face, "Lieutenant Winslow needs to speak with both of you."

Jermaine recognizing the look on Officer Chan's face, "What happened?"

Officer Chan's eyes showed nothing but pain, "I better let Winslow tell you."

Michael and Jermaine's nerves were racked knowing that this had to be horrible news. Just before they got in Jermaine whispered, "Don't speak unless you are spoken to and maybe we'll get through this."

They walked into the office and Lieutenant Winslow was pouring himself a full glass of whiskey. "Sit down." He took a gulp of his drink and then paused, letting it hit him before he continued, "Well, your top suspect is a bust, they were watching him last night and he didn't even leave his house once. I could live with that, we all make mistakes, the reason I am having a glass of whiskey at 9:45 am on a Tuesday is that I had to make phone calls to the families of Officers Malkovich and Lyndon, who were watching Sandra and Cassidy's friend Gloria, and I had to tell their families that they were killed!"

Jermaine's breath was taken away; Michael was also speechless. "This son of a bitch has gone from being a serial kidnapper to a two-time cop killer. The media is going to be up my ass all day and the captain is coming here at 2 pm, you better give me something to work with."

They both left but Michael went back to the locker room and Jermaine followed, just before Jermaine could come through the door Michael yelled, "God damn it!" He punched his locker as Jermaine rushed in and pushed him up against the locker.

"Pull yourself together, we have a job to do." Michael began to struggle, but Jermaine pushed harder, "Listen to me, I have known Lyndon for two years, I have known Malkovich for five years and he saved my life when an undercover drug bust went sideways a few years ago. This is one of the worst days I have had on the job in ten years, I'm pissed too, but punching a locker and yelling doesn't help anything. If you want to be a Chicago PD, take that anger, take that rage aim it at solving this case so that the families of the kidnapped women and the families of the officers can have justice."

Michael settled down realizing Jermaine was right, he paused for a few seconds, "Alright, let me do a little further digging on the Mr. Wells lead and then let's see if anything comes up."

Michael called the gym from his cell phone pretending to be an interested patron, the receptionist told him, "The owner wasn't here last night."

Michael then did a little further investigation on him, "Before he bought this franchise he used to be an electrician."

As he came across that vital information and more, Jermaine came up to him, "Here's what happened last night: somebody cut the power to that block of apartments the whole south side of that floor was black. The only thing we see on the surveillance cameras is darkness."

Michael responded, "I have some news too, our friend wasn't at the gym and he used to be an electrician."

Jermaine's eyes lit up, Michael seeing agreement said, "Let's get a warrant, we have something."

Jermaine paused, "I know you are eager but we have to make sure we have something more than that."

Michael said, "He's not there, we can ask the receptionist to show us around the back area."

Jermaine considered this, "It's a risk, I'm still not sure if he is the guy."

Michael responded, "He's also the vice president of a group called 'Stop the Cops'."

Jermaine's jaw hung open, "Okay, let's go."

They walked in, and spoke to the secretary and asked her where the owner was. She responded, "He went out for lunch, he should be back any minute."

Jermaine told her what happened and asked if they could see the back room. The receptionist got nervous, "Well, I'm not allowed back there, but I know where the key is." The receptionist got it and opened the door just as they walked in, they saw an old van, not the colour of the one in the video but similar.

Jermaine got on the radio, "Please run these plate numbers," and just as he finished giving them, Mr. Wells walked in furious.

"What the hell are you doing here?"

Michael responded, "Investigating the murder of two cops and the abduction of women you have had contact with and didn't keep proper boundaries from."

The man began to fume, "I'm not letting you plant anything on me, get out."

Jermaine responded, "Would you mind telling us where you were last night, Mr. Vice President?"

Mr. Wells became incensed; "Stop the Cops is a peaceful group that is tired of bullies like you getting in our business. Do you even have a warrant?"

Jermaine responded, "Your receptionist let us in willingly."

The gym owner said, "Alright let me sum this up for you two flatfoots, I hate cops it took all my restraint not to throw you off my premises the first time. I was with my girlfriend last night having dinner and a movie, check Chez Jacque's and the theatre on Conner and Talsky. Now if that answers all of your questions, get out!"

Jermaine's radio came back on, "The plates are registered to Mr. Jack Wells and fit the vehicle description."

Jermaine responded, "Thank you."

Mr. Wells pointed at the door Jermaine and Michael left in frustration and temporary defeat.

Jermaine came up to Michael later that day, "Well, Mr. Wells' story checks out, what have you been up to?"

Jermaine looked at Michael who was looking through Facebook, "What are you doing?"

Michael responded, "Looking for some kind of clue, I can't get it out of my head, what did we miss?"

Jermaine paused, "Don't beat yourself up, this case might just be an outlier."

Michael looked back at him, "What do you mean outlier?"

Jermaine leaned onto his desk, "Six years ago a guy walks into a biker bar in Georgia, he looks to the left, he looks to the right and he pulls out a gun that was hidden under his shirt and opens fire. Somebody fired back and he bolted, the cops caught the guy a day later, everyone expected him to be some rival gang member."

Michael got confused, "So if it wasn't that, what was it?"

Jermaine exhaled, "He was targeting people wearing jean jackets."

Michael responded, "Was this guy a fashion Nazi?"

Jermaine said, "No he was someone who thought the world was going insane and wearing the wrong material on the wrong part of your body was part of it. All three of the guys who got shot were wearing jean jackets, so there was a connection it just wasn't where anyone thought it was. I have a report to fill out, make sure you clock out after your shift is done, don't beat yourself up and wear yourself out."

Michael reluctantly said, "Okay."

The workday for Michael and Jermaine had officially ended and Jermaine had been held up talking with a few of the other officers about Malkovich and Lyndon. He decided to make one quick stop to make sure Michael was going to follow his advice, he approached his desk and Michael was staring a hole through the screen as he was typing quickly.

"Michael, I told you to go home when your shift was done, you need your rest."

Michael responded briskly, "I couldn't sleep anyway."

Jermaine pulled up a chair, "Michael, I appreciate your passion and you may not understand because you don't have a family."

Michael interrupted, "Don't remind me."

Jermaine paused for a second confused but then proceeded, "If you get obsessed with this job, it will wear you down and the day may come when you have to deal with a case that can't be solved."

Michael bristled as Jermaine continued, "You have to learn to let these things go or they will haunt you for the rest of your life. Then you might be drinking whiskey at 9:45 am on a Tuesday even when no one died."

Michael didn't respond so Jermaine continued, "Would you stop being so dense, I am trying to help you here, now I have to go home and be with my family. If you want to drive yourself crazy then you are going to do it alone."

Jermaine stood up and began to walk away when Michael spoke, "That picture in your wallet that you are so proud of, imagine what the picture of those women and those officers means to their families."

Jermaine turned around to face Michael again, "I understand but if you do this to yourself you will burn out and then you won't be any good to anybody. What do you think you will find on Facebook?"

Michael responded, "I hope the answer, I can't do nothing." Michael continued to scroll down the page and stopped at a picture of the four of them together. "Jermaine, do you see these women, three of the four are missing and the fourth one is scared to death. I can't just do nothing, if I have to think about every wacky possibility including the fashion Nazi from the bar I will.... the bar." He took a look at the picture in front of him he saw someone in the background.

Jermaine rolled his eyes, "Okay I will give you an hour, after that I will pull you off of that desk if it takes a crane to do it. I have to call my wife and tell her I will be late." Jermaine left as Michael's mind was working at lightning speed.

He began whispering to himself, "Oh my god, it's him, he was the bartender, he talked them up found out their routines, of course, he waited several hours to pass by the cameras outside of when we would be looking for him." Michael called the bar in question and found out that he had quit a month earlier. Michael also found out he had often come to work in a van that fit the description from their case, but was painted yellow. His mind raced as he opened browser after browser getting specific information He took a look at the surveillance footage of the apartment building, "We were looking for Wells so hard that I didn't see who was coming in."

After getting one more intersection camera that showed him pulling into an abandoned factory building, Jermaine came up to Michael, "Are you ready to go home?"

Michael stood up, "We're going. I know where he is." Michael grabbed the keys and ran for the cruiser, Jermaine chased after him.

"Where are we going?"

Michael responded, "We don't need a warrant, he's holding up in an abandoned building; tell the others to stand by if it turns out I'm right."

Jermaine with great concern said, "Okay."

He made the request as they fired out of the station, sirens blazing, to this place that Michael was driven to get to. Jermaine asked him, "Who is he and what makes you think it's him?"

Michael responded, "His name is Luke, he was the bartender at the bar the women went to. The bar owner told me that his van matched the description, the traffic cams several hours after the first kidnapping followed him here. I also have the evidence of him going into and out of the building during the kidnapping of Gloria and the murder of Lyndon and Malkovich. The reason he executed this so well is because he is an ex con and probably took notes from other sick people during his many years in prison." Jermaine was simultaneously impressed and worried that Michael either had a breakthrough or a breakdown.

Michael turned off the sirens as they came close to the property, "Okay, if I'm right he's going to be in there, the women will be too. Then we will have everything we need."

Jermaine said, "Okay, but remember to show restraint, I know you are worked up but I don't want to lose this case due to bad practice." They slowly approached the walled off side of the building, guns drawn.

Michael responded, "Get ready to call it in."

They came closer and closer to the door and instead of a knob it had a metal bar, he pulled on it and thankfully it was open. They went in with guns aimed, over to their left they could hear talking but it wasn't clear. They stepped closer and closer and the voices became clearer, Michael's skin began to crawl as he began to remember that voice he knew only too well. Just as they approached the doorway they heard, the man saying, "If you ever try and escape again I will break more than your jaw and your hand." Michael and Jermaine nodded and got ready to go in.

They burst in through the door to see Luke standing over a tied up and beaten Cassidy as Sandra and Gloria, who were bound and gagged, were looking on. Michael stared a hole through him, "You're under arrest, you murderer."

Luke began running as Michael went after him. Jermaine immediately picked up his radio, "Officers, Michael's suspicions were right, the three victims are here alive please get here ASAP, over." Jermaine began untying them while looking over his shoulder seeing Michael chasing him up the stairs and going just out of view, hoping Michael could handle it.

Michael chased him up the stairs, just as he was close Luke tried to grab his arm, the struggle caused Michael's gun to fall, Luke threw a punch. "You brought this on yourself kid!"

Michael ducked and responded with one of his own that landed, "I'm not a kid anymore."

They were two thirds the way up the metal staircase when Luke kicked his leg and Michael fell back a few steps but had held onto the railing. He quickly recovered and continued his pursuit past the top of the stairs, Luke began to head towards a door leading outside but Michael grabbed him and maneuvered him in the other direction towards one of the abandoned offices. Luke threw another punch that knocked Michael back a step, but Michael charged through and knocked him down with the office door.

With the arrival of the other officers Jermaine raced towards the stairs to help Michael. As he reached the top Michael was on top of Luke who had his hands cuffed behind his back with Michael holding him by the shirt screaming in his face, "I hate you, you ruined everything!"

Jermaine pulled out his gun, "Michael, step away from perp, we got him it's over."

Michael was breathing heavy his face turning red with intensity, he got up and began to walk away. "He's cuffed, get him out of here."

Jermaine began to take Luke towards the staircase when a couple other officers came up to help him prevent Luke from struggling, which he was starting to. The women were being freed and Jermaine walked back towards the police car to see that Michael had moved it so that it would be directly facing the wagon.

Michael had moved over and was now sitting in the passenger seat almost in a trance. Jermaine came into the car and slammed the door, "What was going on in there? There is something you aren't telling me, I saw that look in your eyes you could have killed that guy. I can't have a partner who keeps things from me, especially things about perps."

There was a long pause as the door to the wagon closed with Luke inside. "Okay, they got him, what is going on?"

Michael tried to ignore it, "It's a long story, we got him, we have paper work to fill out, that is all there is to it."

Jermaine yanked the keys out of the ignition, "we are not moving an inch until you tell me what is going on!"

Michael responded, "You don't want to know."

Jermaine blurted out. "The hell I don't, I drove out here two hours after I should have been done for the day, risked my life with partial information, and stopped you from going too far. You are going to tell me everything!"

Michael took a deep breath as the hate in his eyes began to melt away and revealed a deep sadness that was running underneath it. "I um, used to live in Elgin, we moved to DeKalb later on; before that there were four of us, my mother, my father, my younger sister Becky and myself. It seemed like my childhood was going along fine, until one Sunday morning, about 16 years ago my mom was out with her friends, my dad was trying to get me to clean my room and I wanted to watch Justice League. I asked my sister to record it for me, we had our own secret handshake, and at the end we would say 'team Pratt'. A few minutes later my dad was asking my sister to clean her room too, so we were both upstairs, I was almost done…" Michael wiped away a tear that had formed and was falling down his face. "When I heard this loud noise, I opened my door to see what it was and it was him, Uncle Luke, I hadn't seen him in a few years, where he had been was a big secret.

"He took this blunt club and smashed my dad in the head with it knocking him unconscious, before I could process what was happening he had gone into her room and picked up my sister screaming. The only thing I could think of at that moment was that I had to stop him and I tried to stop him. He shoved me to the floor I got back up and ran down the stairs after him. He hit me once in the face with that club, but I was still holding onto his leg so he grabbed me by the head and said 'you brought this on yourself kid' those words are imprinted in my mind. He threw me headfirst into the china cabinet, the glass shattered so fast. When my mother came home, her husband was unconscious, her son was bloody and beaten and her daughter was gone forever." Jermaine listened intently moving to the edge of his seat almost dreading the rest of this story.

"They found him a couple weeks later, but it was too late, she had already been sold into sex slavery who knows where to god knows who. My mother blamed my father for not doing something about his brother sooner, he always responded with 'It's not my fault, my brother is a monster, just like it's not your fault your cousin is a meth head.' After three years of war they divorced."

Jermaine had to wipe away a tear that had trickled out of his own eye, when Michael continued, "When I got older I worked up the courage to try and find out what happens to child sex slaves hoping that maybe she was still alive somehow and one of two things usually happens: either they are sold off to some other horrible people or they just shoot them in the head and replace them with the next victim. It was then that I realized that there was no happy ending for her, that whatever she wanted to be in life was destroyed and replaced with… I never wanted anyone else to suffer the way Becky did."

Jermaine overwhelmed by what he had heard could barely utter a word, "We, we have a lot of paperwork to do tomorrow."

The next day the other police officers were congratulating Michael and Jermaine for catching Luke, Jermaine was happy but Michael wasn't able to enjoy it at all. Around 2 pm the story was shown on the TV declaring that the same two police officers who had broken up the hostage situation at Burger Buster last week had caught Luke Mengels. Other officers were saying to him, "Dude, you did a great thing, you should be celebrating. This guy was a monster and with what you got him booked for he's never getting out."

Michael knew the officer was right but couldn't enjoy the achievement. Before Michael was near the end of his shift when a man came in, asking to speak to him, "Hey are you the cop who busted Luke Mengels?"

Michael, exhausted of thinking and speaking about this ordeal tried to get out of the conversation, "Every investigation is a team effort and no one officer can ever take all the credit."

The man continued, "Yeah, you're him alright, what's wrong with you putting that guy in jail? You should have shot that piece of shit in the head, he doesn't deserve to draw breath. I don't want my tax dollars to protect his life and give that piece of shit food, what's wrong with you?"

Michael, mustering every bit of restraint he had left, said, "Sir the Police Force is supposed to enforce the law not carry out the punishments. That is determined in court by a judge and jury as per the constitution."

This set the man off, "To hell with the constitution! My sister was raped for two and a half days, and got the hell beat out of her, don't you care about what happened!!??" He grabbed Michael's shirt as he was yelling, "She has nightmares, she may never get over it!"

Michael shoved him back his emotion finally giving way, "Get off me…. Be glad you got your sister back, not all of us were so fucking lucky!"

The officers escorted the man out of the station, Michael looked over at Jermaine who had walked in just a few seconds earlier. Michael left for the washroom, where he sat down putting his face in his hands trying to get control of himself.

When he came back out Jermaine escorted him to Lieutenant Winslow's office where the Lieutenant started talking. "Alright Michael, you did something fantastic, you tracked down the evidence and we caught the S.O.B.

However, the truth is that police officers need to be arm's length from the cases they are involved with and if I had even a suspicion that this case involved you personally, I never would have assigned you to it. That being said, Jermaine told me the short version of your history with the suspect Luke Mengels, formerly named Luke Pratt, this situation has clearly awoken some issues that you need to deal with. So, in the interest of helping a police officer who I think has a lot of potential, I am putting you on a leave of absence with pay and we will also be offering weekly counselling to help you work through it. Please go home and when you come back, bring that passion with you to clean up these streets."

Michael left the office feeling horrible, like he had been punched in the stomach, he wanted to be a police officer and now he was being treated like a crazy person. Jermaine tried to talk to him but he said, "I'm sorry, I guess you were right all along. Maybe I'm not good enough to be on this force, maybe I'm just some unstable lunatic that the Lieutenant has to patronize."

Jermaine said, "He wasn't patronizing you, he was actually being nice, you may have to wait a couple years before that happens again."

Michael said, "Fine, nice, caring whatever you want to call it, it won't change what happened 16 years ago and it won't change the fact that I have to live with the fact that I was the only one that could have saved my sister and I failed." Michael grabbed his jacket and left, leaving Jermaine to ponder what he could do, if anything.

Michael went home and he grabbed the picture on his dresser and broke it, leaving the glass protruding through and ripping it. After a few weeks of counselling and time off where Michael just seemed to replay the things that had happened over and over in his head, he heard a knock at the door where Jermaine was waiting in a suit. "Michael, glad to see you."

Michael responded, "Has word spread quickly about what happened to my childhood and now everyone is scared of me wants to transfer me to Australia?"

Jermaine responded, "No, we're doing something that should have been done a long time ago. The car is waiting, come on." They got into Jermaine's car and as they were driving he said, "I spoke to a couple people, I took up a collection and a bunch of precincts chipped in, an officer that takes down a cop-killer tends to be popular."

Michael was confused, "Collection for what?"

However, before he could answer they took a right turn towards the cemetery. "Why are we going here?"

Jermaine responded, "You reminded me what it means to go the extra mile and what it means to care about people you barely know."

Michael rolled his eyes, "Oh no, is this one of those pretend funerals they do on TV for people who are alive to show how appreciated they are, because I don't want people falling all over me."

"Are those some of the guys from the precinct?" Michael asked as they finally approached the site.

"Don't worry about them, this is something that needs to happen."

Michael got out of the car and as they walked to where the other officers were he looked at the name on the gravestone it said, "In Memorial to Becky Beverly Pratt." There was a small casket over the grave, with the top part open with a small red dress with black dots laid in it. Michael was floored.

"That was her favourite dress, it reminded her of ladybugs, she wore it in the picture I have at home."

Jermaine responded, "Your mother held onto it after all these years."

Michael's emotions were welling up inside him, Jermaine said. "I'm not a psychologist but you have been holding onto this for 16 years, I want you to look at right in that coffin and say whatever you need to say to start moving on with your life... I'm serious, talk!"

Michael approached the casket as the emotions began to pour out. "Hi Becky, it's been so long, I, I'm sorry, I'm sorry I couldn't save you. I'm sorry that you suffered for years and years and that you probably died in a horrible place, you deserved better, much, much better."

He took a long pause, "I felt that guilt for so long, wondering if only I had done this or if only I had done that, I could have saved you and I could have stopped Mom and Dad from divorcing, maybe there was nothing I could do, I was a ten-year-old boy. I did do something though, I stopped Luke from sending more women to where you were sent, he's going away for the rest of his life and maybe if I fight hard enough I can help give others what you didn't get... a real chance at life. I love you and I always will." He put his hand over the right sleeve of the dress and lightly moved it around for a couple seconds and said, "Team Pratt." He closed the casket lid.

The tears flowed out of him as the casket was gradually lowered, he and Jermaine had an emotional embrace, and together with the other officers who were there they all picked up a shovel and helped him finally begin putting the past to rest. As the grave was filling up Michael looked to his right at Jermaine and suddenly remembered that next to the shattered torn picture of his shattered torn family was a new picture that he had taken on his first day on the Chicago police force of him and his new family

CONCLUSION

Thank you all for reading.

I hope this gave you plenty to think about and if it reached you in a deeper way outside of being simple entertainment whether it be intellectually, emotionally or both, then I have succeeded. I look forward to writing for you and other people in the future, I have plenty of ideas left and from the bottom of my heart, thank you for reading and letting my voice be heard.

Made in the USA
Charleston, SC
23 November 2016